Carsten Bothe

Dutch Oven

Cooking Over an Open Fire

Schiffer Publishing Ltd
4880 Lower Valley Road • Atglen, PA 19310

PUBLICATION

Published by Schiffer Publishing, Ltd.
4880 Lower Valley Road
Atglen, PA 19310
Phone: (610) 593-1777; Fax: (610) 593-2002
E-mail: Info@schifferbooks.com

For the largest selection of fine reference books on this and related subjects,
please visit our website at **www.schifferbooks.com.** You may also write for a free catalog.

This book may be purchased from the publisher.
Please try your bookstore first.

We are always looking for people to write books on new and related subjects.
If you have an idea for a book, please contact us at
proposals@schifferbooks.com

Schiffer Books are available at special discounts for bulk purchases for sales promotions or premiums. Special editions, including personalized covers, corporate imprints, and excerpts can be created in large quantities for special needs. For more information contact the publisher.

In Europe, Schiffer books are distributed by
Bushwood Books
6 Marksbury Ave.
Kew Gardens
Surrey TW9 4JF England
Phone: 44 (0) 20 8392 8585; Fax: 44 (0) 20 8392 9876
E-mail: info@bushwoodbooks.co.uk
Website: www.bushwoodbooks.co.uk

Library of Congress Control Number: 2012947879

Originally published by: Heel Verlag GmbH as *Dutch Oven* in 2011
Text: Carsten Bothe
All Photos: Carsten Bothe and Buechsenmacher-Verlag archives
(Jens Kollmorgen and Will Hocker)
With the exception of [C] iStockphoto: pp. 21, 137
Setup and Formation: Claudia Reinierkens, reinierkens kommunikations-design, Cologne
Editor: Petra Hundacker
Translator: Dr. Edward Force
Designed by Mark David Bowyer
Type set in Optima BQ / Humanist 521 BT

ISBN: 978-0-7643-4218-9

--All statements without guarantee--

Printed in China

The methods and instructions in this book have been carefully worked out and checked by the author and publisher. Since they will be used without the influence and control of the author or publisher, we—the author and publisher—have no liability for or guarantee against personal, material, and financial losses. Use the book at your own risk!

Carsten Bothe

Dutch Oven

Cooking Over an Open Fire

FOREWORD

Dear Readers,

A cooking pot is a cooking pot, but a Dutch oven is more—it is a symbol of the Wild West, of freedom and adventure, of good food from a campfire, of independence, and life in the world of nature. Cooking with a Dutch oven has become a movement that brings people from all over the country together and lets them become friends.

Plunge with me into the world of the trappers, cowboys, and pioneers from the land of unlimited possibilities, or conjure up dishes from an open fire for your family and friends as a pleasant change from typical grilled foods.

The experiences of dozens of cooking courses and hundreds of hours at the cooking fire have contributed to this reworked new edition. As for the recipes, you can start by assuming that they work. You can get the ingredients at your local supermarket, and your local butcher knows the cuts of meat. And the dishes really taste good! Not only because they are just naturally good, but also because the Dutch oven gives a certain tasty tang to the food, thanks to its untreated cast iron.

Meanwhile things have happened to the Dutch oven: You are now equipped with preparation that creates a sort of patina and makes pre-warming unnecessary. One cannot improve more, and more does not need to be improved anyway.

Now, there is not much more for me to do than to wish you a happy glow under the pot, and, as always, I am happy to receive praise or serious criticism.

Heartily yours,

Carsten Bothe

America's Original Cookware.

October 17, 2002

Dear Reader,

We extend congratulations to Carsten Bothe on this new book converting traditional German dishes into camp Dutch oven recipes to share with other Dutch oven cooking enthusiasts.

The history of the Dutch oven dates back to the Renaissance along with the art of casting pots and kettles. Tight fitting lids began to appear for the kettles and pots by the mid-eighteenth century. Further refinement followed and a "camp oven" or "bake oven" was developed not only for use at the hearth but for use at a campfire.

With the development of newer and more sophisticated kitchen appliances, the interest in campfire cooking declined. In recent years, however, Dutch oven cooking has enjoyed a revival in the American West and throughout the world. Now we are seeing renewed interest in the tradition, pleasure, flavor and mystique of "the old black pot magic."

We are grateful to Carsten for all he is doing to spread the word about Dutch oven cooking.

Sincerely,

LODGE MANUFACTURING COMPANY

Bob Kellermann
Chairman and CEO

BK:gag

Enclosures

Side Dishes

Bread and Rolls

Cake

Various 156

Dessert 169

In The Beginning ...

Do you remember your grandmother's old kitchen? Perhaps there was still a big oven there that was heated with wood. If so, then your grandmother definitely hung heavy cast-iron pots in the fire-holes. Perhaps you can still remember the special flavor of the foods: delicate, juicy stew roasts and wonderful, tasty casseroles...

The younger folks among you have probably been told often that Grandma's kitchen was something very special, with a flavor experience that nothing could equal. Surely that was because, for one thing, your grandmother was an excellent cook. But one should not disregard how the foods were prepared then—in heavy cast iron pots! And those pots became more and more valuable by being used over the years.

Now these traditional pots are coming back, after traveling a long way across the ocean and through the land of unlimited possibilities. The Dutch oven was the cast iron cooking pot that went on the great settlers' treks. Thus the old iron casseroles from Germany became a part of American cuisine.

In our highly technical and fast-paced lives, more and more people are looking for balance with the simple things of life. Cooking and eating together rank among the most important rituals of human fellowship. When one combines this with the original outdoor life, a campfire or a picnic, it can become an unforgettable experience for children and adults alike.

The nice thing about the Dutch oven is that you can set it up anywhere, not just where an open fire is allowed. Grilling sites are equally suitable when you heat the Dutch oven, not with the glow of a fire but with charcoal briquettes. The choice of foods that one can prepare in a Dutch oven is also much more extensive than, for example, by grilling. When friends meet at the fire after a day of hiking, or simply gather on the terrace and everybody puts his Dutch oven on the fire, one can be sure that it will be very pleasant.

And after foods have been cooked up in a Dutch oven, one becomes so eager for more that Dutch oven fans will not be put off from using them outside, even by the weather...

The History of the Dutch Oven

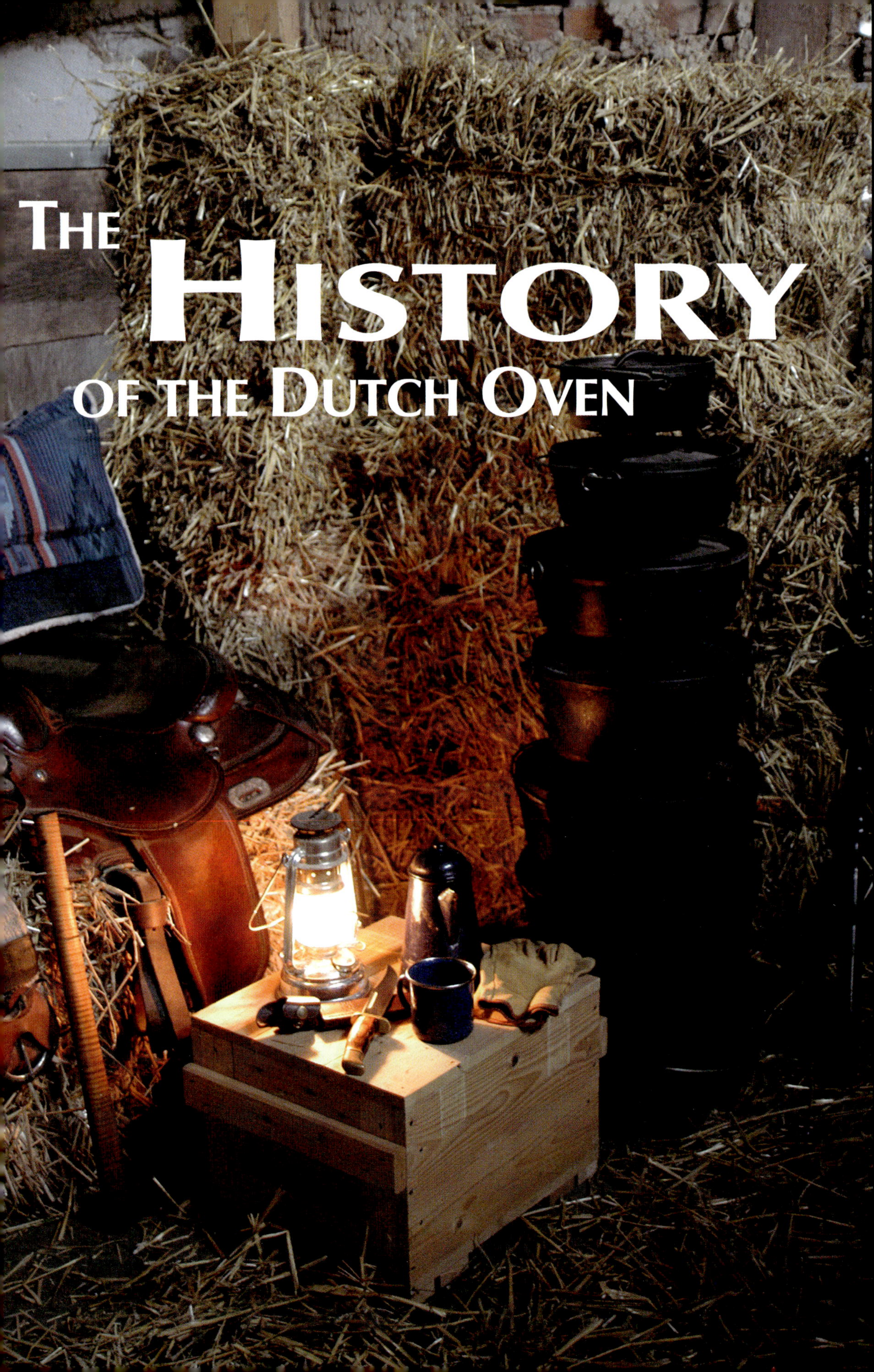

A Personal Experience

Perhaps you would be interested to know how I came to bring the Dutch oven to Germany. In any case, the story is worth telling.

Going hunting with the trappers, sitting by a fire in the endless vastness of the Rockies—that was what I wanted. And a Dutch oven was simply a part of it.

I bought my first black pot in the wilds of Wyoming and brought it to Germany in my hand luggage. I still have it today. And whenever I cook in it, my thoughts turn back across the prairie and through the snow-covered woods to coyotes, martens, bears, and elks.

One day my work called me to Frankfurt and the ambience of a large consumer-goods fair. I visited the fair on its last day, and in one of the rearmost halls, standing at a small booth, was Bob Kellerman, grandson of the Lodge Manufacturing Industries firm's founder, amid Dutch ovens of all sizes!

The first Dutch oven in Germany.

I had already tried to import Dutch ovens into Germany, but only the personal contact and the shared enthusiasm for the fascination of Dutch ovens made the business link complete.

My ten-year old Dutch oven is, for me, not only a cooking utensil, but also a friend with which I have had many adventures and spent many nights at a campfire. That's why it is so exciting.

The Lodge Cast Iron firm has already been in business in the USA for more than a century. With the 1896 founding of the firm that produced these old cooking articles of heavy cast iron, Joseph Lodge saved a piece of American history that had already reached the promised land with the Mayflower in the form of big black iron pots.

Joseph Lodge, the firm's founder.

Bob Kellerman, the present director, in the fifth generation.

Why Are the Black Pots Called "Dutch Ovens"?

The Dutch oven has accompanied Americans through the centuries and is described again and again in historical accounts as the most important utensil of the great trek that moved westward in the early eighteenth century.

For the first settlers too, the Dutch oven was essential. Peddlers handled their distribution then. These peddlers came from the ethnic group called "Pennsylvania Dutch." "Dutch" is now regarded as meaning "from Holland," but we now know that the settlers in Ohio and Pennsylvania were of German origin. The similar sounds of "Dutch" and "Deutsch" seem to have led to a misunderstanding that has not been cleared up to this day.

At that time, owning a collection of cast iron cooking utensils was very costly, so much so that "cast iron kitchen furniture" was regularly included in last wills—for example, in the will of George Washington's mother Mary.

The Life of a Cowboy

The Dutch oven traveled in the chuck wagon, the cooking wagon that accompanied the great treks and cattle drives. Many will know chuck wagons, and also Dutch ovens, from motion pictures about cowboys. In fact, many hungry cowboys were fed with Dutch ovens. For all those who had to camp beneath the sky for a few days, there were versions of Dutch ovens made of lighter sheet steel or aluminum. But working with those types was much harder, and frequently the sheet-metal lid melted into the beans in the heat of a cowboy's campfire before the beans were cooked.

Back at the base camp or on the ranch, every cowboy looked forward to his place by the fire and the food from the heavy Dutch oven—and all the rest waited eagerly for the flavored account of each cowboy's experiences while they gathered around the fire and ate.

The Significance of the Dutch Oven Today

Whether on a trek, a cattle drive, herding sheep, prospecting for gold or serving in the cavalry, the Dutch oven was always there for you. For Americans, life under the open sky always played a special role. It is firmly linked with our history. Camping and cooking outdoors with all the refinements of a kitchen thus holds a high value in modern America too. It is not the privations of olden days that one would like to relive with a Dutch oven; it is the awareness of the old values, the close contact with others that characterized settlers and cowboys and brought them together. They not only depended on each other, but treasured togetherness as something very valuable. Sitting around an open fire, hearing sung or narrated ballads of fast shooters or wild horses, and emptying a black pot of beans and bacon together in the process, that was, and is to this day, part of the American way of life.

The quality of cooking in cast iron pots is also known so well in the USA that there are rustic, country-style restaurants in which cooking is done only in Dutch ovens. There are also cooking shows and television chefs who practice Dutch-oven cooking. Outdoor cooks regularly recognize their masters in great Dutch-oven cooking competitions that take place in Utah, where the International Dutch Oven Society (IDOS) is located.

A cowboy cook around the turn of the century.

THE HISTORY OF THE CHUCK WAGON

In 1866, rancher Charles Goodnight of Texas was faced with the problem of having to feed his cowboys on the cattle drive to the north. Until then, every man had cooked his own food, but there was not enough time. Thus, he took an old, mustered-out army wagon and attached a chest with various drawers to the back end. This chest closed with a flap that could be opened downward and, resting on a table leg, used as a work space. As simple as the idea was, it revolutionized the American cattle industry.

A chuck wagon from the turn of the century.

A modern cook with his chuck wagon.

The cooking utensils were kept in the drawers; in the barrel on the side was a two-day supply of water. In the front part of the wagon were the cowboys' bedrolls and raincoats, plus other tools and supplies.

The name of the chuck wagon comes from "chuck," a piece of meat from a steer's shoulder, which is cheap and tough and thus was typical cowboy food. Thus the cooking chest was called the chuck box and the whole field kitchen the chuck wagon.

While the trail boss was in charge of the herd, the cook was the undisputed boss in his realm. And he had another important job: Every night he turned the stem of the chuck wagon to the North Star, for on the prairie there is scarcely an orientation point. If the herd stampeded in a panic, one at least knew the right direction in the morning. Even today, many Americans follow this tradition by parking their trailers with the hitch to the north.

The cowboys' menu was monotonous, rich in fat, and poor in vitamins; life was hard and consumed strength. The main ingredients were beans, bacon, rolls, and gravy; the cowboys could only dream of juicy steaks. For the night rider, the cowboy who watched the herd at night, there was always hot coffee at the campfire, and a hearty soup was bubbling in the Dutch oven.

OLD COWBOY WISDOM:

**BREAKFAST WAS BEFORE SUNRISE
AND SUPPER LONG AFTER SUNSET.
I THINK THE COOK HAD SOMETHING TO HIDE,
SINCE WE ALWAYS HAD TO EAT IN THE DARK.**

CHUCKWAGON ETIQUETTE

. Nobody eats before the cook releases the food!

. If the cook hoists a white flag, there are women in the camp, so behave yourselves properly!

. First eat, then talk!

. It is OK to eat with your fingers; the food is clean!

. If you pour yourself coffee and someone calls “Refill,” you must refill everybody!

. Don’t spit in the pots!

. Eat with your hat on!

. No refills before the cook allows!

. No horses near the chuck wagon!

. Ride downwind to and from the chuck wagon!

. Whoever comes back to camp must bring firewood. Nobody comes with empty hands!

. Bring the dishes to be washed!

. Strangers are always welcome!

Preparation and Care of a Dutch Oven

The heavy weight of a Dutch oven tends to disguise the fact that the black pot needs care and is not "unbreakable." Cast iron is extremely brittle. Even a Dutch oven won't survive a fall onto solid ground.

The cast iron of a Dutch oven is porous. This has the advantage of giving food in a long-used pot a very special taste. This flavor patina is just as desirable as the flavor of a good tea from an old teapot with a layer of theine from long years of use.

One must never disturb this porous material with strong cleansers. The soap substances would be picked up by the material and could be given off into the food during cooking.

Burning In

So that such a thing cannot happen, the Dutch oven must be burned in before its first use. The Original Lodge Dutch Ovens are already burned in at the factory. Thus, they can be used to cook at once. But if poor care or thoughtless lending to a careless friend destroys the patina, the pot must be burned in again.

To do this, it is first dipped in hot water and dried. Then the entire surface—still hot from the warmth of the water—is rubbed with neutral-flavored plant fat ... Coconut oil is very well suited to this. The warm material sucks the fat up very well. Thus prepared, the empty Dutch oven is put in the home baking oven upside down and left there at least an hour at 280 degrees. Then one turns off the oven and lets it and the Dutch oven cool. After this procedure, the fat can be rubbed in again with a kitchen towel. The Dutch oven is clearly darker, and instead of the gray color, it has taken on a dark brown tone. In this procedure, part of the fat evaporates and beclouds your kitchen under some conditions. Thus do not leave the Dutch oven alone when you are burning it in, and ventilate the kitchen well!

Alternatively, you can carry out this procedure outside in a grill, which will get hotter than an oven and thus better form the patina, and also does not smoke up the kitchen.

Without this initial treatment, the Dutch oven would give off a metallic taste from its production to the first food cooked in it. It would also take up the flavor of the first food and give it off to the next. It would be quite unsatisfactory if a sweet dessert suddenly tasted like chili.

Burning in is best done on a grill in the garden.

This treatment fills the pores of the metal with neutral-taste fat and protects the cast iron from rust. You should repeat this treatment regularly. Cook fatty foods in the Dutch oven the first time, if possible, but not any foods with much acid, such as tomatoes or cherries.

Cleaning and Care

The Dutch oven takes on a black patina from use. This is what once gave the black pots their name. You must preserve and protect this. It is iron hammer oxide, the same substance that forms in forging. It is an iron oxide that forms only in heat and, unlike normal red rust, gives the foods a smoky flavor.

As with other cast iron utensils, the cleaning of a Dutch oven is especially important. You must never treat the cast iron with soap or other cleaners, as the porous material will take in the soap materials and the soap will remove the protective layer of fat. This layer is important to prevent food from burning while cooking. Through regular use and the right cleaning, you get a cooking pot in which nothing burns and that is very easy to clean, with water and nothing else!

To clean, just wash your Dutch oven out with hot water. If foods have dried on, then put the pot with the water over heat and let the water boil. Most of the food can be scrubbed off with a brush; in very stubborn cases a scouring pad of rust-free stainless steel helps. One can also use some salt as a scouring aid, but then the fat layer is destroyed and your Dutch oven must be greased anew and, if necessary, be burned in again (see previous instructions).

With normal use, it is usually sufficient to wipe out your Dutch oven with a kitchen washcloth.

A stainless steel pad and hot water suffice, even with the coarsest dirt.

STORAGE

If you would like to store your Dutch oven for a long time, then you should grease it with a good cooking oil and put a paper towel inside it to absorb any moisture. It helps to prevent stuffiness by not quite closing the lid. If you have not used the pot for a long time, you should check before use to see if the fat has turned rancid.

You should never store food in your Dutch oven, above all any acid-intensive foodstuffs. At the contact surface of food, pot, and air, red rust forms constantly, spoiling the food and damaging the pot. After cooking, remaining food should immediately be moved to a bowl.

It is very bad if you let the pot stand outside with ashes on the lid and it rains. The salts and other constituents of the ashes will surely cause the lid to be rusty the next morning.

Here is another important tip: Never pour cold water into a hot Dutch oven. It would cool unevenly, warp, and no longer close tightly.

When you have oiled the Dutch oven, you should wipe the fat off roughly before cooking, especially on the rim of the lid, for if you later apply heat to the fat, it will begin to smoke, and bake the ashes with the lid and the fat.

With a brush you can even get the oil into the lettering, which is hard to reach.

You can remove the last bits of food with a scraper.

It is best to transport a Dutch oven in a wooden box. Put a kitchen towel in the pot to absorb moisture.

About the Recipes ...

We have tried to keep the recipes as simple as possible, so they will be suitable for the Dutch oven as a pot for outdoor cooking. Thus, some of the recipes include only vague quantities. Then too, not every recipe can be limited to a certain size of Dutch oven. In that case, we have noted it, but unfortunately, not every recipe could be cooked with every pot size—that would have exceeded our budget and life expectancy! Simply experiment, tasting the recipes again and again while cooking.

For abbreviations, we have used "TSP" for teaspoon and "TBSP" for tablespoon.

Cooking with a Dutch Oven

Dutch ovens can be had in various sizes.

What Is a Dutch Oven and How Does it Function?

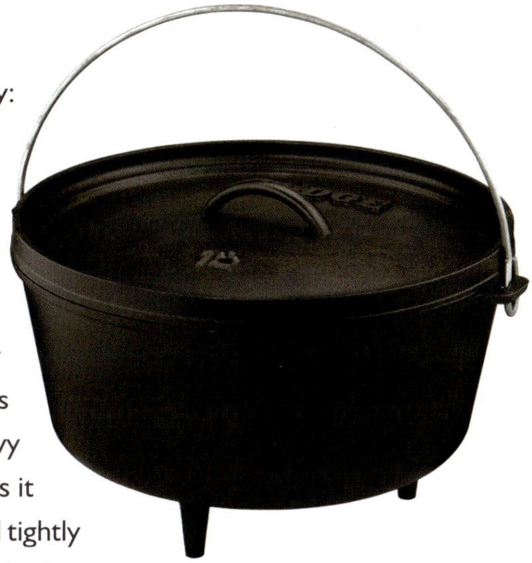

These questions are explained easily: The Dutch oven is a heavy pot of cast iron with a precisely fitting lid. The Dutch oven is made in various sizes with diameters between 8 and 16 inches, plus some in deep and shallow versions.

The massive cast iron heats the foods inside slowly and protectively. Once heated, a Dutch oven needs remarkably little fire for the cooking process. The heavy material evens out the irregular heat of a fire and passes it on gently to the food. The ridged lid keeps the pot closed tightly through its weight and exact fit. Thus, the foods cook in their own heat, much as they do in a pressure cooker. As a result, meat becomes incomparably tender and juicy.

A Dutch oven is fitted with three legs, so that the heat source can be pushed under it. Why only three? Very simple: three legs never wobble!

The lid has a raised rim, so that the heat applied to it never falls down. Thus the Dutch oven is heated from all sides.

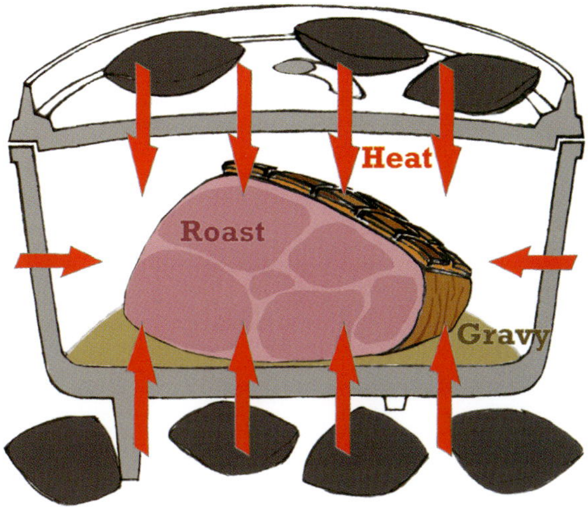

The lid is simultaneously a frying pan. It is put on a trivet for this use, with the upper side down, and heated with a few coals. Thus steaks, bacon, eggs or pancakes can be fried.

The functioning principle of a Dutch oven, with heat from above and below.

The Basic Equipment

To cook with your Dutch oven, you need just the Dutch oven with the lid, a lid lifter, a trivet, very heat-resistant protective gloves, and—naturally—a small fireplace with charcoal briquettes and tongs. For all those who did not learn to cook something in the Boy Scouts, the use of a charcoal starter is recommended. This is a small oven that resembles a piece of stovepipe. This starter or igniting chimney is filled from above with charcoal briquettes and perhaps an igniting aid, and lit. With these brilliant little devices, anybody is able to heat briquettes. As soon as the briquettes begin to turn white, they have the right temperature and can be used for cooking with the Dutch oven.

The old trappers could naturally not use modern grill briquettes, so they had to use glowing pieces of wood, or dried buffalo chips on the treeless prairie. The techniques that worked a hundred years ago have surely not gotten any worse, but why not use the modern products? Inexperienced users of Dutch ovens should certainly use briquettes since they can very easily and precisely heat the Dutch oven. They can also be used to determine the temperature in a Dutch oven very easily. As a rule of thumb, the number on the top equals the number of briquettes to be placed above and below. Since those briquettes below heat better, you can take three pieces away from those below and add them on the lid. A Dutch oven with a 12 on the lid thus gets 12 + 3 = 15 pieces on the lid and 12 – 3 = 9 below. With this arrangement, the Dutch oven reaches about 175 degrees. It is a common beginner's error to pack the oven with heat above and below. The cooking result is then usually meager, black, and unenjoyable...

Which Size is Right?

Oven Size	Contents	Portions
6	1 quart	1-2
8	2 quarts	2-4
10	4 quarts	4-7
12	6 quarts	12-14
12 deep	8 quarts	16-20
14	8 quarts	22-28
14 deep	10 quarts	22-28

The portions listed in the chart refer to a full plate—but remember that a hungry cowboy takes two or three portions. It is better to work out the size you need on the basis that one quart of pot volume suffices for one person. You need not fill a pot to the brim, which means that more liquid can be put into the deep pot than into the flat model of the pot that is one size larger. Another error made in choosing a Dutch oven revolves around the fact that the 16 size is intended for baking, and not for making soup as is often attempted. You should not cook any fluids in the 16, since it tips and turns over easily when picked up, spilling the contents.

For your first equipment, you should get a deep 12 and then a 10 for a family of four people. Plus a lid lifter, coal tongs, and a pair of heat-resistant gloves. Then you can start!

What Else Is There?

Naturally, the pot itself is essential for cooking with a Dutch oven. But the Lodge company also has several useful "helpers" in their offerings, and they will be covered briefly here.

Probably the most practical tool for a Dutch oven is the **Lid Lifter.** Of course one can also use a tree branch, but the lids of the larger pots are very heavy. When they are hot, one quickly notices that they can be removed from the pot and replaced only with great difficulty, especially if one needs to stir the food inside with the other hand.

Lid Lifter

Lid lifter in action: It holds the lid firmly.

Even the largest Dutch-oven lid is held firmly by the crossbar, so you can remove it from the pot easily and without problems. It is especially convenient that the lid is guaranteed to remain perpendicular with the lid lifter. This makes sure that no coals fall into the food. Thanks to its length, one stays far enough from the hot pot so that it is not necessary to put on heat-resistant gloves every time you look into the pot.

Some people lift the lid with the hook at the end of the scoop, which is also possible, but less safe. If you improvise, then take a hammer with a point, such as roofers use. This hooks firmly under the handle of the lid and also prevents uneven loading of charcoal, which makes the lid tip.

So that the lid of a Dutch oven may become a practical frying pan for bacon, eggs, pancakes, and other such foods, it is best to use a **Trivet**. It can be used for all sizes of Dutch ovens, and can be stored in a small space because it folds. Of course, stones or wood blocks can also be used, but it is hard to balance the lid evenly on them. When you prepare juicy steaks, you certainly do not want to hold the lid in place with one hand, but want to have both hands free.

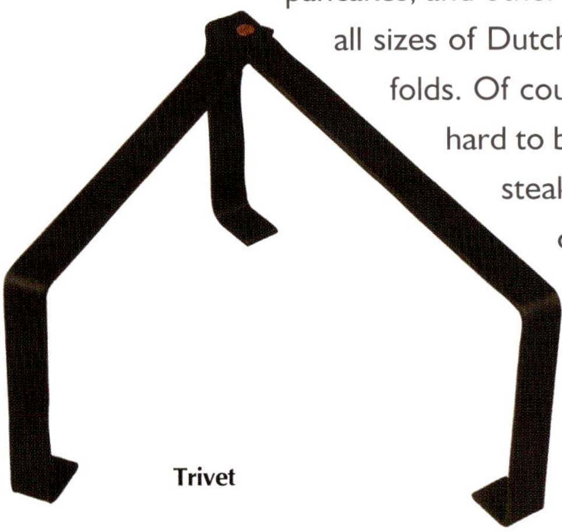

Trivet

In the chapter on the care of the Dutch oven, you learned that it should be greased inside and out with cooking fat from time to time to protect it from environmental influences and guarantee a certain neutrality of flavor. That means that the Dutch oven is usually a bit greasy. How can you transport it best without getting everything else greasy?

The lid is turned over on the trivet for frying.

Several manufacturers offer suitable carriers. But they have not proven themselves, since they cannot be stacked or stored safely in a car. The best thing to do is to make **simple boxes of practical wood.** They can be stacked, and things can be set aside on them when you cook outdoors.

A home-made wooden box for a Dutch oven.

Have you thought about how to place the charcoal precisely on and under the Dutch oven? You need **Coal Tongs** for this.

They should be long enough to let you keep a sufficient distance from the heat, light weight, and easily used with one hand.

Many Dutch-oven cooks try to use worn-out grill tongs. They work, but you should then cook only where a hot coal can fall safely to the ground. This will certainly happen when you use charcoal briquettes. Those little round things are hard to pick up with tongs that have only two jaws. The Lodge charcoal tongs are better suited. They are made of rust-free stainless steel and are very light. They also have regular gripping jaws. Thus the round briquettes can be placed safely on and under the Dutch oven. The spring mechanism on the joint of the tongs makes working with heat very simple.

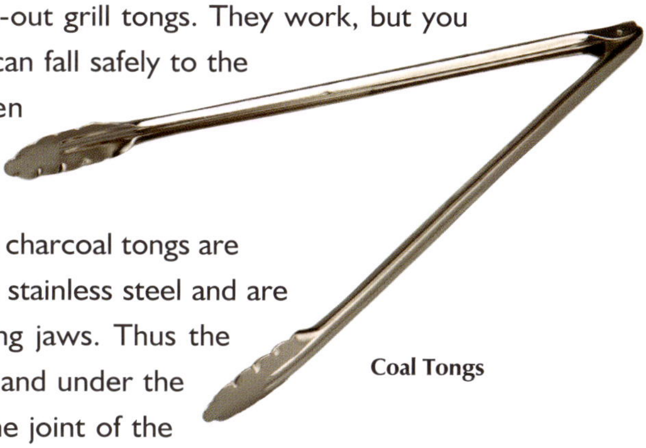

Coal Tongs

To remove the ashes from the lid, you can use an **Artist's Brush.** These wide, practical brushes are easy to find on the market.

You can sweep the ashes away with an artist's brush.

For working with a Dutch oven you should always have a pair of **Heat-resistant Gloves** lying ready. You can, of course, move the lid easily with the lid lifter. But if you are cooking with several pots at the same time and want to place them one over the other to save charcoal, it is best to wear gloves. The Lodge firm offers very thick wild-leather gloves among its products. They protect you from high heat and yet are so soft that you can easily grip smaller objects too. Welders' gloves, available on the market, are also suitable. But remember that the insulation of the gloves only works when they are dry and clean. As soon as water or oil gets on the gloves, the heat is transferred inside them.

Note that when cooking with gloves, you do not notice if they begin to burn and by then it is too late to take them off.

Heat-resistant gloves are a must!

To light the briquettes quickly and simply, the **Charcoal Starter** in stovepipe form works well. Here the briquettes are poured into the top of the starter (on the grid). To light them, one or two pieces of newspaper, crumpled, and placed underneath, and then lit, will do the job.

After ten minutes, flames come out of the top and the coals are glowing almost all the way through. Then you simply take them out, one at a time, with the tongs, and use them for cooking.

Left: Charcoal starter–the ideal device for igniting charcoal briquettes.

Right: the coals are soon glowing.

The Fire Site

The Dutch oven is so designed that you can use it wherever an open fire is allowed. You can even use a Dutch oven well on a simple garden grill, as long as the grill can hold the weight of the pot. You need only remove the grid from the grill and put the pot in the bowl of the grill. The legs of the Dutch oven are long enough to let the coals fit underneath.

A field smithy is an ideal device for cooking with a Dutch oven. The United States offer the greatest assortment of Dutch-oven cooking sites at outdoor cooking events. Curious contraptions, brilliant ones, and sometimes a whole folding kitchen can be seen at these events.

But, a small level surface of 20" x 20" on the ground is really enough. A simple fire site consists of four bricks and an old baking surface, such as can be found on junked stoves.

On a field smithy there is enough room for up to three Dutch ovens side by side.

A Dutch-oven table with a windbreak—there is really nothing better.

The upper heat of the lower pot is also the lower heat of the upper Dutch oven.

The universal fire site as a table for cooking.

But if you do not like to bend, you should look at the American "way of cooking." We Americans like to build grilling tables for light transport, on which one can work with a Dutch oven while standing. The upper steel plate should be at least 5 mm [0.197"] thick. Thinner sheets bend easily under the heat of the coals. Under the grill plate, it is best to have a grid that folds and gives the grill plate added stability. The dimensions of the grill table depend on the number of pots to be heated at one time. A longer grill table, on which two or three pots can stand side by side, plus a lid as a frying pan and a grill, is naturally very inviting for garden parties with many guests. But one can prepare food for a remarkable number of guests on even a smaller grill table, since the Dutch ovens can be stacked and heated.

It is also very easy to use the lid as a frying pan. Whoever does not have a trivet (previously mentioned) can set two or three concrete blocks in a semicircle and lay the lid on them.

The lid is ideal for frying—here, tasty mushrooms.

The advantage of a Dutch oven is that its season does not end when bad autumn weather begins. At least not for those who have an open fireplace. What can be nicer than coming home after a walk in the cold winter air to a fireplace with the aroma of a hearty casserole wafting from it.

If you improvise a fireplace outdoors, or want to cook with your Dutch oven on, for example, a canoe tour, then you should remove a grass divot and put it aside. Later you can lay the grass back on the fire site and thus disguise it.

For cooking on a fire, there are some things to remember:

- **Surround the fire site with stones to limit it. But remember that some types of stones can explode in a fire, especially quartz (silex) and stones that have long been in water.**

- **When cooking with charcoal on a campfire, you should select a site for the fire and then, some distance away, make a place where you cook on the coals that you take from the campfire. When you cook on a campfire, you must make sure that you turn the pots every few minutes, since the radiant heat of the fire heats one side of the pot and can scorch the food at the rim.**

- **Also make sure that the Dutch oven rests on flat stones or really flat ground. Otherwise the legs may sink into soft sand and the pot will lie right on the glowing coals. These will be pushed into the sand and soon go out for lack of oxygen.**

- **To be able to cook properly on an open fire, you also need a small shovel to put coals on the pot lid. Unfortunately, a lot of sand also gets onto the lid.**

Coal shovel

If you cook for some time at a fixed place, you should build a small fireplace: Build up a knee-high wall, brace it with wood, and position the cooking fire on top. Now you no longer need to bend down.

Whoever wants to set up a cooking corner in the garden can also use old bricks, stacked loosely without mortar. With such a fireplace one no longer needs to bend down and cook uncomfortably.

A raised fireplace of dry stacked bricks.

Naturally, you can also cook with a Dutch oven in a very normal garden fireplace from the hardware store.

Many campfire cooks try at first to cook with a Dutch oven on a tripod. Although it works, this is not very practical. With flat pots, you should make sure that they do not easily overflow and spill when you cook something fluid.

The most elegant solution for cooking with a Dutch oven is a fire-resistant table. I use a field smithy for this. Also well-suited is an old baking sheet, placed on a normal table with four bricks.

With a Dutch oven, you can cook in a garden fireplace.

A tripod is not very practical, but is suitable for using a Dutch oven.

HEAT REGULATION

The Dutch oven actually regulates the heat itself. Through its great mass, it spreads the point of the fire's uneven heat, allowing for even cooking. Aside from that, one naturally must control the fire or glow so that the heat reaches the right places.

First of all, a brightly glowing fire is much too hot for cooking. A flame is also unpractical because the pots get sooty and are hard to clean. The layman always imagines that a pot must hang on a chain over a glowing fire, and that the flames almost meet above the pot's lid. This is, above all, not practical. Just imagine that you want to remove the lid to stir the food. With all that heat near the pot, this would be a very unpleasant task. It is better to work over glowing coals.

Instead, there are grill briquettes that are not as stylish but much more practical. They can be grasped easily with tongs and placed exactly where the heat is needed. Ten briquettes under a size 10 Dutch oven suffice to cook the contents. One can even fry in fat. First try cooking with these briquettes and be sure that they supply more than enough heat. If you set the pot in a glowing fire, the contents will soon char.

With grill briquettes, heat regulation is child's play.

When you choose grill briquettes, do yourself a favor and buy Kingsford. They cost more, but glow like a good cigar and leave only white ashes. Cheaper briquettes always leave a lot of dirt and stones behind on the surface, and unconsumed bits of wood in them will smoke. The big supermarket chains deal with briquette producers who are concerned not with quality, but only with the price. These dealers buy on the world market and have the goods filled into bags. Thus you can never be sure after you have had good results if the next bag will be of the same quality.

Naturally you can also cook with the heat of a campfire—that has been done for hundreds of years—but you need some experience. It is simplest when you pile up thumb-thick dry pieces of wood for a fire, light them, and let them burn. The remaining heat is ideal for cooking and baking.

When you plan to bury the whole pot in a heap of coals for a long time, for example when you start a bean dish in the morning for eating in the evening, then you should burn only arm-thick wood.

First of all, the coals should no longer burn, but only glow; second, they should not be too close to the sidewalls of the pot, and never under the pot, but only lie on the pot lid. The food in the pot must also be damp enough not to be baked.

With a campfire, the biting smoke is often a nuisance, but dry wood reduces it to a minimum. Then too, only the pieces that still want to burn, but from which the flames had been blown out by the wind, make smoke. Simply put these pieces back in the campfire and blow on them if need be, to make them burn again. The smoke will stop right away.

If you would like to cook on a campfire, we recommend that you produce the heat in a fire and continually remove the embers for cooking… A small coal shovel is handy for this. With a folding spade, you take too much sand, which gets shoveled onto the lid of the pot.

The heat for the Dutch oven is produced in the fire beside which it rests.

How to Set the Right Cooking Temperature

You can determine the temperature in your Dutch oven very simply by first heating with grill briquettes.

The upper heat can be set very well by the number of grill briquettes.

The quantity of required briquettes can simply be taken from the following reference table. The upper number in every row is the necessary grand total of coals. But they are divided unevenly. Because of spreading upper heat, there must be more coals on the lid. In the lower row of the table, the first number stands for the number of coals on the lid, the other for the number of coals under the Dutch oven.

To reach, for instance, 370 degrees Fahrenheit with a size 10 Dutch oven, you must put 16 of the required 23 coals on the lid and seven under the oven.

Size	Temperature 320°F	345°F	375°F	400°F	425°F	455°F
8	15 10/5	16 11/5	17 11/6	18 12/6	19 13/6	20 14/6
10	19 13/6	21 14/7	23 16/7	25 17/8	27 18/9	29 19/10
12	23 16/7	25 17/8	27 18/9	29 19/10	31 21/10	33 22/11
14	30 20/10	32 21/11	34 22/12	36 24/12	38 25/13	40 26/14
16	34 22/12	36 24/12	38 25/13	40 27/13	42 28/14	44 30/14

TIP!

When you roast foods like goulash or chopped meat, always cook only a small quantity at one time, or else the Dutch oven will cool off too much and the meat will be cooked, not roasted.

A Few Tips on Outdoor Cooking

One can cook with a Dutch oven anywhere. But naturally, there is a difference between being on your home terrace and wanting to end a day's hiking with a hearty dinner from a Dutch oven, far from any kitchen comforts.

It is obvious that some dishes are better suited for an outdoor event than others. Sometimes it is just a little bit of extra work right before preparing a dish that drives one to multiple improvisations and despair. For example, when the recipe requires putting the finished meat in a prepared bowl with a skimming ladle, because the needed sauce has to be beaten strongly with a whisk so as not to have any lumps.

Before four people take the meat out of the pot with pocket knives to set it in a cap, one should check the recipe in advance as to its outdoor suitability.

For simple recipes that are well suited for cooking far from civilization, you will find an appropriate hint.

A Word About Cooking Times ...

If one uses the specified number of briquettes for one's Dutch oven, the cooking times can agree very well with the data in this book. But there are many small details that can influence the cooking time, thus all time citations begin with "approx." (approximately).

If the Dutch oven is partially exposed to the wind, the cooking time can be a little longer, because the oven keeps cooling off. If it is really stormy, the wind can fan the coals and the food gets done far sooner or even burns.

If you put the Dutch oven on loose sand, the pot may sink in and put out the fire.

It gets very challenging if Dutch-oven cooks want that smoky aroma in the food. Cooking on a wood fire requires a lot of experience, as it is usually too hot for Dutch-oven cooking and is always hard to regulate.

Note than when you want to try out a recipe from a "normal" cookbook, the cooking times will be clearly shorter in a Dutch oven.

TIP!

A roasting thermometer is a necessary device. With it, one knows the cooking status inside.

With a roasting thermometer, you can determine the attained temperature inside a roast.

The Subject of Liquids ...

Every cook knows the problem of "cooking dry." Unnoticed, the liquid in the pot has cooked off and the stew has cooked fast to the bottom of the pot. Naturally, you must check the fluid level in a Dutch oven now and then. But the problem of sticking fast does not occur as often as, for example, in a stew on the stove, since the pot is firmly closed. Thus, the liquid is kept a long time, much as in a Roman pot. This is also the reason why a Dutch oven stew is so juicy and tender.

In principle, it does not matter whether you use a deep or normal Dutch oven. To be sure, you should make sure that in cooking some dishes, such as gratin, a lot of upper heat is needed. This is easier to do with the same volumes of foods in a larger but flatter Dutch oven than in a deep one with a similar capacity, since the coals on the lid are nearer to the foods and thus more upper heat occurs. Besides, the crisp and tasty surface is larger and more people get some of it.

The volume and the surface also play a role of some forms of bread baking. A flatter bread in a flat Dutch oven is finished sooner and regulated better than a thicker lump of dough in a deep Dutch oven

Many Hungry Guests

The Dutch oven is very suitable for filling many people quickly under the open sky.

If a long line of hungry friends awaits you at the Dutch oven in the country, then you should have that in the back of your mind when you choose the foods and plan a meal that can be eaten with a fork or even a spoon, for the plate must be held with the other hand. Then too, the food should be heavy and hot (and stay hot a long time)—and meat should be seen. For nothing is more annoying then finding a green salad on the plate first when your stomach is empty—cold, light and without meat—the whole mood is ruined!

A big bowl of hearty pea soup, chili con carne, or stew is better, and with it, a slice of thick, gray bread, and the world is in order. Since the food is so hot, the guests must eat slowly, and the feeling of satiation comes on sooner.

TIP!

Guests should put a folded napkin under their plates so they don't burn their hands.

Some Means of Estimating Portions:

- **Hearty soup or stew when hunting or after a whole day of paddling: about 3 cups per person (3 soup spoons).**

- **For meat, 7 ounces per person (if women are there too and there are many side dishes), for students or similar types, 10½ ounces fresh weight are not too much, not even 14 ounces.**

- **For whole animals with bones (small pigs, chickens), 28 to 35 ounces fresh weight.**

- **To compare: 3½ ounces of mortadella (Italian cured sausage) equals five slices.**

The Earth Oven

In America we also discovered the earth oven. It is also called a bean-hole and is intended for slow-cooking bean dishes. The hole is dug two handbreadths deeper and wider than the pot and lined with stones.

To heat it, a fire is burned for two hours, until there is significant glow and the stones are white hot (over 300 degrees).

After two hours half of the coals are removed from the hole and the pot of beans or chili is put in.

The traditional ingredients are dried beans, no matter what color or kind. Then bacon, brown sugar and/or molasses, salt, pepper, and mustard powder. Tomatoes do not belong in this dish.

The beans are put in at least two hours before eating, but they are better left overnight. A good ratio of bacon and beans is one part bacon to two parts dried beans. Besides bacon, smoked pig's knuckles or other pork are suitable.

I always smoke the pork as long as possible and then let it dry slowly. It is only meant for baked beans or pea soup.

A Simple Earth Oven (Bean-Hole)

For a deep size 12 Dutch oven, you can build a functioning and durable earth oven easily.

You need only three square feet of open, flat ground. You set your Dutch oven on this clear patch and stand bricks on end around it two fingers distance away to mark the size. Mark the outer contours of the bricks on the ground and dig the bricks in, still standing on end. The bricks will end even with the ground level. A slight tilt to the outside makes sure that the bricks do not tip over. An old cookie sheet or the cover of a kitchen stove serves as a cover. Now the earth oven is finished!

Baking Beans in an Earth Oven

The earth oven is not very simple to use, but whoever gets used to it does not want to do without it.

First, set a fire in the hole and hang the Dutch oven with the beans over it on a tripod to cook. After two hours and regular stoking, the hole should be half-full of glowing coals. The beans are now soft and you can sample them. The fluid should now be a finger-breadth above the beans, or preferably a little less.

At this point, the Dutch oven goes into the hole. Take half to two-thirds of the glowing coals out of the hole and put them on the overturned cookie sheet. Then sink the Dutch oven with the beans carefully into the hole so that it stands level and the distance to the edge is the same on all sides.

Now fill the coals back in so that the space between the Dutch oven and the wall of the earth oven is filled. Put the rest of the coals on the lid. It helps to attach a chain to suspend the Dutch oven firmly to the handle. Then you can remove the pot better, since you can simply pull it.

Now you must cover the bean-hole with the sheet. This is best done by pushing the rim of the cookie sheet into the ground. The trick is to smother the fire by cutting off the air. The beans should cook in the heated earth oven and not in the fire, which would be much too hot.

Use several bricks for sealing, to hold the rim of the sheet down, and also seal the edges with poured-on earth to prevent rising. It also helps when you have removed the coals from last heating and add them on top of the fresh coals until the earth oven is filled.

Observe the rim of the sheet. If smoke still rises somewhere, the fire is getting oxygen and burning too hot. Even the next morning there is still plenty of heat that can be blown into a fire. In other words: The beans are then in the middle of the fire for twelve or more hours. That has also happened to me. The result was a centimeter-high layer of ashes in the Dutch oven, where I thought the beans were.

As for the bean-hole, it is important that the beans are already almost done when they go into the earth oven. Their time in the earth oven is only supposed to spread the aroma better and make the beans mealy. Thus there is no exact time for how long the beans must remain in the oven. The longer, the better. It is best to cook the beans in the evening and bury them in the oven; then they are finished in the morning.

1. The finished earth oven with the bricks as its wall.

2. Start heating it properly!

3.

4.

5.

6.

7.

8.

9.

10.

5. Shovel half the coals out of the hole and set the Dutch oven in it.

6. Fill the hole with the hot coals and–if there is room–with ashes.

7. Cover the earth oven. If it is still smoking, that must be stopped.

8. When it is properly covered with earth, no more smoke rises.

9. This is how the baked beans look after two hours in the earth oven–tasty!

10. This is the traditional form of a trapper's breakfast.

In no case should you—no matter how curious you are—open the oven every two hours to see what the beans are doing. Every time it will lose some heat, and the results are in danger.

Opening the earth oven is at least as exciting as opening Tutankhamun's grave!

In The Morning

To open the earth oven, you should wear fire-resistant gloves and have a folding spade and hand brush ready. First remove the bricks from the sheet and then the sheet itself. The oven should still contain lukewarm coals.

Remove enough ashes from the hole so you can pull the Dutch oven out of the hole by the chain. In no case should you try to take the lid off the Dutch oven while it is still in the ground. If you did, ashes would fall into the beans.

When you have lifted the Dutch oven out of the hole, remove the ashes from the lid with the hand brush. Then take off the lid and enjoy those beans!

Other foods that need a long cooking time can also be prepared in a bean-hole, such as goulash, cabbage dishes, or stews.

Recipe

For a Deep 12" Dutch Oven		
4	oz.	white beans (or quail beans, kidney beans, or a mixture of them),
2		dried onions, cubed
1	lb.	bacon
2	cups	brown sugar
2	tbsp.	fresh-ground mustard
1	tbsp.	pepper, freshly ground in coffee mill with the mustard
		salt for seasoning (after the beans are cooked!)

Let the beans soak in water the night before and make sure they are always well covered with liquid. The more the beans are soaked, the less water they take in during cooking, so you can adjust the liquid better.

Cut the bacon into coarse strips and fry in a deep 12 Dutch oven over the earth oven. Also fry the onions. Then add the beans, the ground mustard, and pepper, plus the brown sugar, and mix well. The liquid should be two fingers above the beans, since a lot of liquid will be lost. When cooking them over the fire, add water frequently. In no case should you salt the beans before they are cooked, since then they won't get soft (obviously, *but better safe than sorry*!). Over the fire, cook the beans about two hours until they are soft. Then season and salt them. Don't put on any more wood now, and let the fire die down.

Softened beans.

Bean Baking Process

Evening before:	Soften beans in plenty of water.
Morning:	Soak the beans now; check that a finger's breadth of water is over the beans.
4:00 PM:	Heat the earth oven with hardwood, gathering the wood ashes from the last use in a pail for later reuse, if you want.
4:30 PM:	Hang the Dutch oven over the earth oven on a tripod. Fry the bacon and onions. Then add beans, mustard, pepper, and sugar.
6:00 PM:	Beans should be done. Now salt and season them; let the fire go out.
6:30 PM:	Shovel about ¾ of the glowing coals out of the earth oven and put on a sheet. Carefully lower the pot into the earth oven and scatter the glowing coals over it. If there is room in the pit, you can fill it with the ashes from last time. Then press the cookie sheet into the ground and cover its edges with earth.
Next morning:	Remove the sheet and carefully take out the pot. The contents should still be warm enough to eat.

Dutch Oven Brisket

Brisket, the English name for beef breast, is the star of the BBQ, for this tough, firm flesh must be cooked for hours to make it enjoyable. While in Germany brisket is traditionally prepared as soup meat; in the USA it is cooked in the smoker for at least twelve hours.

What could be better than using an earth oven to cook this cut overnight, left completely to itself? Through the long cooking time, the connective tissue becomes gelatinous and the meat can be easily chewed. And the flavor of the sauce is incomparable!

1.

2.

3.

4.

5.

6.

Recipe

For a 12″ Dutch Oven		
4-6	lbs.	brisket, excess fat removed
2		large onions
		grilling spices to choice
1	cup	sweet ketchup
		some oil for browning

Heat the earth oven with hardwood pieces for two hours. Season the meat generously with the spices you choose.

When the earth oven is almost burned out and half full of coals but with few flames, brown the meat strongly on both sides over the fire in the earth oven. Add the onions and ketchup to the meat.

To bury the pot in the earth oven, first remove half the coals, put the Dutch oven in the earth oven and pour the rest of the coals over the Dutch oven. Then shake the wood ashes from the previous use into the earth oven until it is brim-full. Then cover the earth oven with a cookie sheet and seal the edge with sand so no more smoke rises. You can dig out the Dutch oven the next noon and enjoy a still-hot lunch.

1. Ingredients: Brisket, seasoning mix, onions, and BBQ sauce.
2. Rub the meat with the seasoning.
3. Put the meat in the Dutch oven with the quartered onions and pour the BBQ sauce over it.
4. Brown the meat well over the earth oven.
5. An earth oven with a good bed of coals looks like this!
6. The Dutch oven is dug in and the earth oven sealed.
7. On the next day a wonderful aroma rises from the Dutch oven!
8. The meat is wonderfully aromatic and soft as butter.

7.

8.

The Dutch oven is especially well suited for preparing meat, since it cooks in its own steam, thanks to the heavy lid. Besides, the meat can be browned in the Dutch oven and then stewed further.

To do this, simply heat some olive oil in the Dutch oven and brown the meat from all sides. Then pour some water, broth, or wine on it. Thus the meat stews in its own juice with the lid closed. Some onions, celery, and carrot pieces are excellent additional flavor carriers.

Use a roast thermometer to find out when the meat is done inside. It is stuck into the meat and shows the inner temperature. This varies much, depending on the type of meat, to cook the meat through.

MEAT

Pork Roast

A pork roast is ideal for an introduction to cooking with a Dutch oven. This is a pork roast with skin, which can be purchased very reasonably from a butcher or market.

Cut a grid into the meat with a sharp knife and pepper the roast. Put it in a suitable Dutch oven. Add two quartered onions, some pepper, and a cup of water.

You need not brown the meat first. Cook the first two hours with very little upper heat until the roast is done. Then add lots of fresh coals to the lid. The upper heat makes the rind brown and crisp.

For six pounds of meat you need something over two hours. Serve the roast cut up on fresh rye rolls.

The trick is to finish cooking the roast first and then make the crust crisp.

1. Cut a grid in with a sharp knife, then pepper it.
2. Put in the Dutch oven along with the vegetables.
3. Check the inner temperature with a thermometer.
4. After cooking, prepare the crust with much upper heat on the roast.

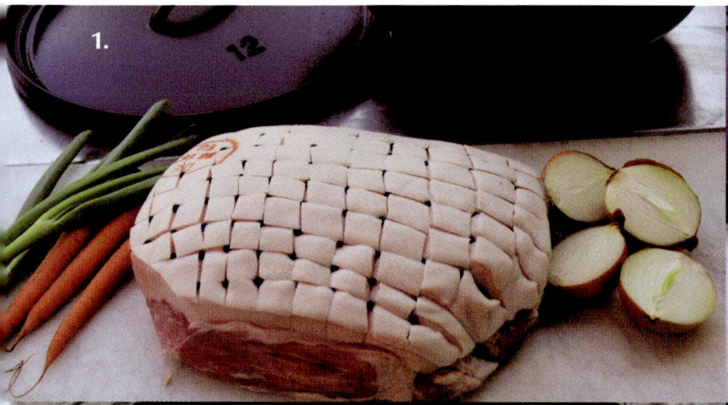

Veal Shanks

For four people		
1		veal shank (3 lbs.) cut into four slices by the butcher
6	tbsp.	clarified butter
3		onions
2		large tomatoes
1		carrot
¼		celery stalk
		garlic, 1 clove or powder (to taste)
¼	tsp.	rosemary and sage
		parsley
		lemon juice
1	cup	meat broth
½	cup	beer (dark beer gives a seasoned sauce)
		pepper and salt

Season the veal slices with salt and pepper and brown ten minutes on each side in clarified butter. Cube the vegetables; cook the tomatoes in advance so the skins can be removed. Quartered canned tomatoes are also suitable.

Add the cut-up onions, celery, carrots, tomatoes, and the garlic clove pressed in salt, and steam, turning constantly.

Add the meat broth and beer. Add the rosemary, sage, parsley, and a good squirt of lemon juice.

Close the lid and let stew 50 to 60 minutes with upper heat. The cooking time depends somewhat on the thickness of the veal slices. You should also regularly make sure that the bottom of the Dutch oven is covered with fluid, and add some broth if needed.

Sides: Fresh white bread for dipping, but in any case a nice cool beer.

Rhenish Sauerbraten

For four people

2	lbs.	beef shoulder (original would be horse meat)
4	tbsp.	clarified butter
2	cups	beef broth
1	tsp.	sugar
1	tsp.	mustard
1	cup	fresh or sour cream
3	drops	Tabasco
1	squirt	Calvados
		Some black bread, best pumpernickel

Pickling:

2	cups	red wine, not too dry
2	cups	water
3	tbsp.	balsamic vinegar
		salt
1		handful raisins
1		carrot
1		onion, quartered
3		cloves
3		laurel leaves
¼		stalk celery

Mix all the pickling ingredients, boil, and let cool. The Sauerbraten is put in this mixture for 2 to 3 days.

Melt the clarified butter in the Dutch oven and brown the roast, seasoned with salt and pepper, in it on all sides. Then fill with some of the pickling and the ingredients, pumpernickel, and broth. Let it stew a good 70 minutes. When the roast is done, take it out and keep it warm on the lid.

Season the sauce with salt, pepper, sugar, mustard, Tabasco, Calvados, and perhaps more pickling. Stir in the cup of fresh cream and serve with the carved roast.

Sides: Noodles, potatoes, dumplings, and a nice cool beer.

Fillet Tips in Calvados Sauce

For four people

4		medium pork fillets (one per person)
2		small apples
		clarified butter
1–2	cups	sour cream
		pepper and salt
		Calvados

This dish is simple and easy to prepare, since all the ingredients can be prepared in advance. Cut the pork fillets into strips, season with salt and pepper, and brown well in clarified butter. Add the sliced apples and steam briefly. Then stir in the sour cream, season with salt, pepper, and a good squirt of Calvados, and serve with dumplings.

Veal Fricassee in a Pot

For four people

2	lbs.	veal (breast or shoulder)
		Butterschmalz
1		onion
		asparagus pieces from a can (some 14 oz.)
1		carrot
		parsley
		lemon juice
½	cup	meat broth (instant)
1	tbsp.	flour
		pepper and salt

Cut the meat into bite-sized cubes, season with pepper and salt, and brown in clarified butter. Add the cut-up onions, carrot, and parsley, and steam for a moment. Finish it all with a good squirt of lemon juice. Mix the flour into the broth and add to the fricassee.

Let it all stew for about an hour with the lid closed, checking the liquid regularly, and adding more broth if needed. At the end of the stewing time, add asparagus and warm up.

Ribs

- Thick ribs with bones, approx. 1 pound per person (have the butcher cut it) or spareribs
- Fat for frying
- Barbecue sauce from the bottle
- Honey for brushing

This recipe is outstanding and can be prepared very easily. I don't care for spareribs myself, as there is very little meat on them. So I prefer thick ribs cut into pieces along the bone.

Brown the meat in hot fat in the Dutch oven, coat with barbecues sauce, and let it heat for an hour. When the sauce has become creamy, brush the ribs with honey and brown another ten minutes with much upper heat. The ribs should be so soft that the bone can be twisted out.

If you have a second Dutch oven, you simply must bake fresh bread.

1. Thick ribs with onions are layered in the Dutch oven and browned.

2. After browning with a honey glaze, the ribs are ready.

With spare-ribs, this dish is a joy for people who like to nibble.

Roast Venison

For a 10 or 12 Dutch Oven		
3	lbs.	venison shoulder (or beef)
2		onions
2		carrots
1		chili pepper
		pepper and salt
		fat for frying

Brown the peppered and salted meat well from all sides in a Dutch oven. Add two cubed onions and one carrot cut into crude pieces. If you like it spicy, add a small chili pepper.

Fill the Dutch oven with water until the meat lies two fingers over the liquid. Close the lid and stew one and a half to two hours.

Before serving, the sauce can be thickened with flour.

Lamb Stew

For four people		
2	lbs.	thin lamb shoulder (or even fillets)
5	tbsp.	olive oil
3		onions
1		garlic clove, crushed
		parsley
		fresh lemon juice (or dry white wine)
		some paprika powder (mild)
1	cup	sour or fresh cream
½	cup	broth
		pepper and salt

Cut the lamb meat into small strips and season with pepper and salt. The fat should be removed carefully, since lamb fat always has an unpleasant waxy taste.

Brown the lamb pieces in olive oil. Add the cut-up onions and garlic and steam briefly. Add broth, lemon juice (or dry white wine), and chopped parsley, and stew some 20 minutes.

Then stir in a cup of sour or fresh cream and season again with salt, pepper, and some paprika powder.

Sides: Sliced potatoes, pita bread or olive bread.

Hungarian Venison Ragout

For four people		
2	lbs.	venison
½	lb.	large white beans
2		red paprika peppers
2		onions
1		garlic clove
¼	lb.	bacon
		butter for frying
		some thyme and parsley
½	cup	broth
		fresh cream
		pepper and salt

Soak the white beans overnight to soften them and cook in the soaking water until done. Season the cubed venison and brown along with the bacon. Add the cut-up onions, garlic, thyme, and coarsely cut pepper and steam briefly. Then pour on the broth and let warm for some 30 minutes.

Finally mix in the prepared, drip-dried beans and warm.

Before serving, garnish with a few pepper strips and a little fresh cream.

Shish Kebab

This is a very simple recipe that overwhelms you with its very delicate results. Choose the Dutch oven by the size of the meat.

Pork neck roast without bones, ½ to ¾ lb. per person.

Onions

Roast seasoning

Sunflower or (even better) olive oil

The neck roast without bones is cut in coarse rings and placed in a paste of onions, oil, and spices. For two pounds of meat, use 1 pound of onions. Mix the oil with the store-bought roast seasoning until you get a thin, flowing paste that is mixed with the onions until the individual pieces of onion are well stuck. Brush the roast with the rest of the liquid and turn it again in the seasoning that remains stuck to the meat. A very thick roast should be cut lengthwise so the seasoning can penetrate to the inside.

Put a layer of onion-oil-spice mixture in a glass bowl (plastic can be discolored), lay the roast on it and spread the rest of the onion mixture on the roast and, if possible (see above), in the middle of the cut. It is advantageous if the bowl is so small that there is almost no space between the roast and the edge of the bowl.

1. The seasoned roast with onions in the marinade.
2. The roast is done after two hours!

1.

2.

Thus prepared, the roast is marinated in the refrigerator for a day, although two days won't hurt. The roast should be recoated carefully every four to six hours, so the oil can spread anew.

For roasting, remove the onions from the outside; they can remain in the cut; and brown from both sides in a very hot Dutch oven. Oil is not needed, since the meat still has enough oil from the marinade. Then add the onion-oil-seasoning and brown with it.

Before putting the lid on, add a cup of water per two pounds of meat, or the roast could scorch.

An hour is needed for the first two pounds of meat, another 45 minutes for the next two pounds, and another 30 minutes for every additional two pounds. Thus a six-pound roast must be roasted for two hours and 15 minutes. But a roast should not be heavier than 6 pounds. Thus, it is recommended that a heavier roast be divided.

Sides: The sauce with the stewed onions,
Rye rolls, white cabbage salad,
Beer and marching music.

At left is the pork roast, at right the rye rolls in a deep 14 Dutch oven.

1. Cut the ingredients into slices.
2. Season the meat and make alternate layers of bacon and onions in the Dutch oven.
3. Pour a cup of steak sauce over the filling.
4. The layered meat is done when the first pieces are brown.
5. Layered meat tastes best in a fresh roll.

Sliced Meat

Sliced meat is a Dutch Oven classic par excellence. The recipe is not only incredibly easy, but you can also experiment with the spices and the steak sauce.

For a 10 Dutch Oven		
5½	lbs.	pork neck, cut into slices
		steak seasoning
2–3		large onions
15	slices	smoked bacon, cut approx. 3 to 4 mm thick
1	cup	steak sauce of your choice, or smoky ketchup

Season the pork-neck slices, cut the onions into slices approx. 5 mm thick and make alternate layers with the bacon in the Dutch oven. The layered meat should be built up firmly.

Finally, pour ketchup or steak sauce over it all. This is the only liquid; the rest forms from the meat juice and onions.

Lamb Stew

For a 12 Dutch Oven		
1	lb.	cubed lamb meat
8	cups	water
6	cups	chopped vegetables of your choice
1–2	cups	beef broth
4	tsp.	Worcestershire sauce
1	cup	wild rice
		some lemon zest and maybe some fresh fruit
1		laurel leaf
		thyme, oregano, tarragon
		pepper and salt

Put the lamb meat, water, vegetables, broth, seasoning, and Worcestershire sauce in the Dutch oven and warm it all in water. Then simmer for one and a half to two hours, until the meat is tender. Add the rice and bring it all to a boil. Simmer until the rice is done.

Roast Pork Rolls with Sunflower-Herb Stuffing

For a 12 Dutch Oven		
4	lbs.	pork neck
½	lb.	sunflower seeds
1	bunch	each of fresh parsley and marjoram
3		garlic cloves
¼	lb.	ground parmesan
½	cup	meat broth
1		onion
1		carrot
		pepper and salt

Separate the bones. If you want, they can be added to the sauce later. Cut the meat horizontally deep enough so it can be pulled apart. Rub salt and pepper in everywhere. Chop 1/2 cup of sunflower seeds, herbs, and peeled garlic in a mixer or by hand. Mix the cheese and some broth into a paste that can be brushed on. Spread half the paste onto the meat. Roll up the meat and tie in a roll with string.

Brown the roast well in the Dutch oven, then stew 15 minutes at 250 degrees with the bones, the remaining broth, the peeled onion, and the carrot. Then, reduce the heat and cook gently for some 90 minutes. Toward the end of the cooking time, roast the remaining sunflower seeds on the upside-down lid of the Dutch oven. Now coat the roast with the rest of the paste, scatter the roasted sunflower seeds over it, and bake ten minutes with plenty of upper heat.

Sides: Potato dumplings, bread or mixed salad.

Lamb Ragout

For four people		
2	lbs.	lamb shoulder
6		garlic cloves
4	tbsp.	oil or 50 grams butter
1	lb.	shallots
2		carrots
2	stalks	celery
1	sprig	rosemary
1		laurel leaf
		pepper and salt
1½	cups	hot meat broth
2	tsp.	ketchup
½	cup	red wine
½	bunch	smooth parsley

Cut the meat into walnut-size cubes. Heat the oil in the Dutch oven and brown the meat from all sides over high heat. Peel the shallots and carrots and cube fine; peel the garlic and chop small.

Melt the butter in the lid of the Dutch oven, steam the shallots, garlic, and carrots in it three minutes and add it all to the meat. Clean the celery, cut into rings, and add to the meat along with the herbs, broth, and ketchup.

Cover and stew about an hour, stirring now and then. Ten minutes before the end of the cooking time, add the red wine. Season the ragout, remove the rosemary and laurel. Wash the parsley, pat dry, cut coarsely and scatter over the meat for serving.

Venison Ragout

For four people		
2	lbs.	venison (ribs, neck or blade)
1		onion
¼	lb.	bacon balls
2	tbsp.	cranberries
		fresh chanterelle mushrooms
		venison seasoning
		pepper and salt
1	cup	cream
⅔	cup	venison juice or water

Cut the meat into ¾" – 1" cubes and brown in the Dutch oven along with the bacon and seasoning. When the meat is already brown, add the onions and brown lightly. Fill with ⅔ cup of water or venison juice from a jar, add cranberries, and stew 45 minutes with upper heat.

Brown the mushrooms in coconut oil in the lid (it gets very hot!) and add just shortly before serving.

Now and then check the fluid level in the pot and add liquid if necessary.

Add the cream before serving, then the browned mushrooms, and heat briefly. Season again if you want with salt, pepper, seasoning, cranberries, and a squirt of cognac.

Stuffed Peppers

For a 12 Dutch Oven		
8		big green peppers (should fit into the pot)
2	lbs.	chopped meat
2	tbsp.	olive oil
2		medium onions
2	tsp.	salt
1	tsp.	pepper
½	tsp.	cross cumin
½	tsp.	oregano
½	tsp.	cumin
1	tsp.	garlic powder
		several squirts of Worcestershire sauce
1	cup	rice for the peppers, 1 cup of rice as a side
2	cups	puréed tomatoes from a can or pack
1	cup	water

Remove the seeds, stems, and white walls in the middle of the peppers.

First cook the rice in the Dutch oven. For the peppers you need one cup of rice in an uncooked state; more rice is naturally needed to serve as a side. Thus you should prepare another cup of rice per person. As soon as the rice is done, take it out of the Dutch oven and keep it warm.

Then brown the chopped meat strongly in olive oil in the Dutch oven and add the finely chopped onions. Season it well with salt, pepper, cumin, oregano, garlic powder, and several squirts of Worcestershire sauce. Add about one cup of the cooked rice. Stuff the prepared peppers with this and put them in the Dutch oven, add the pureed tomatoes and the water, and stew about an hour at 180 degrees. Before serving, remove the stuffed peppers from the Dutch oven and add the cooked rice, to heat it briefly in the sauce.

Put one of the peppers on each plate and serve with rice and tomato sauce.

Red Pepper Meat

A chili that is mild enough for children. For eight people.		
1¾	lbs.	kidney beans, soaked overnight, or 3 big cans
3¼	lbs.	beef (goulash meat), cut into small cubes
½	lb.	rib bacon
5		large onions
5		green peppers
5		hot peppers
3		large cans peeled tomatoes
		olive oil for frying
		chili powder
		pepper and salt

Brown the cubed onions and bacon balls in the Dutch oven. Brown the meat, one portion at a time, in the lid of the Dutch oven and then put it in the Dutch oven. Add the kidney beans and soaking water to the meat, cover, and cook one hour with low heat.

Then add the cubed peppers and hot pepper rings. Cook again for half an hour. Then add the tomatoes after cutting them in pieces in the can with a long knife. Season the peppered meat strongly with salt, pepper, and chili powder.

Side: White bread.

Stewed Lamb Shoulder with Red Wine

For a 12 or 14 Dutch Oven, depending on the size of the shoulder		
1		lamb shoulder
6		shallots
4		garlic cloves
		olive oil
1	sprig	rosemary
1	sprig	thyme
⅔	cup	dry red wine
1	cup	lamb juice
		pepper and salt
1	tsp.	flour
1	tsp.	butter

Halve the shallots and peel the garlic. Brown the lamb shoulder well all around in olive oil in the Dutch oven and then take it out of the pot. Steam the shallots and garlic, add rosemary and thyme, and pour in red wine and lamb juice.

Now salt and pepper the shoulder, then put it in the Dutch oven and stew approx. 45 minutes at 150 degrees. Take out the herb sprigs, crush the shallots and garlic, or better, strain them. Mix butter and flour, put the lamb shoulder aside briefly and unbind the sauce with the flour and butter. Then soak the shoulder about two minutes with it.

Sides: rosemary potatoes or bread.

Potjiekos (Small Pot Food)

A traditional dish from Namibia, which is prepared on the beach there

- Meat (simple, low-priced pieces are suitable: lamb, beef, venison, pork, etc.)
- Vegetables in season (potatoes, beans, corn, onions, zucchini, tomatoes, peppers, etc.)
- Oil for frying
- Plenty of red wine
- Pepper and salt
- Seasoning to taste (curry, chili, coriander, etc.)

This dish is quick to prepare but needs a long cooking time, at least four hours.

Brown the goulash-sized cubes of meat well in oil in the Dutch oven. Layer the small-cut vegetables over it and season every layer with pepper, salt, and the other seasonings. The top layer should be potatoes.

Fill the pot with red wine and let it simmer with just a few coals under the Dutch oven.

Look into the pot now and then, not because it helps, but because it makes your guests think you know what you are doing! If too much wine evaporates, then add some.

Spend the time until you dine with the rest of the red wine.

Sides: Rice, white bread, or the corn mush known as Mieliepap.

POULTRY

Poultry with Vegetables

A very simple dish, as if made for a Dutch oven. Depending on the size of the pot and your appetite, you need one or more roasting chickens (3 lbs.), pheasants, doves, or…

Put in the pot for every bird	
2	onions, quartered
1	pepper, cut into strips
2	potatoes, cut into small pieces

If you like, you can add a corn ear, canned corn, or any vegetable you have on hand. The exact quantities do not matter very much in this dish.

Salt the bird inside and out, sprinkle with chicken seasoning if you want. Put olive oil in the Dutch oven so the bottom is covered. Pour in some water if the poultry is very dry, and lay the birds on their backs in the pot, then add the vegetables. Salt and pepper the whole thing, and add a few chili peppers if you like.

The Dutch oven can be left to its own devices with plenty of upper heat for an hour to an hour and a half. Then it is important that there is enough fluid in the pot, so that nothing burns. The bird will not become crisp, to be sure, but rather wonderfully tender and juicy.

1. The bird lies on its breast and the backbone is removed.

2. Thus, one can lay the bird flat on its back.

3. With vegetables, the bird is baked until it is done.

4. The finished product on the plate.

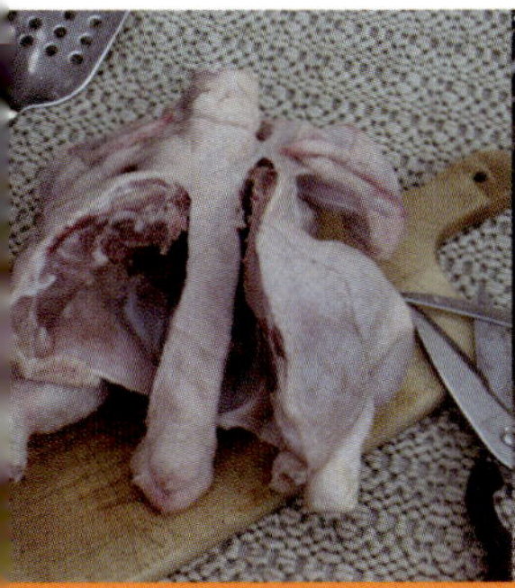

Pigeon Pot

For four people		
2		pigeons
1		day-old roll
1	cup	milk
1		large onion
1		carrot
		parsley
1		egg
½	cup	butter
¾	cup	champignon mushrooms
½	cup	broth
½	cup	white wine
8	tbsp.	whipped cream
		pepper and salt

Take out the pigeons, wash, pat dry, and season with salt and pepper inside and out. Cut the onion, carrot, and parsley small and steam several minutes in the butter on the lid.

Break up the roll softened in milk and knead, along with the egg, salt, pepper, and cooled vegetables, into a firm mass.

Stuff the pigeons with this material and put them in the Dutch oven, breast up. Add broth, white wine, and butter flakes plus the mushrooms cut in slices, and stew approx. one hour with the lid on and upper heat. Check the fluid regularly and add some broth if need be.

Take out the finished pigeons and halve for serving. Pour the pot juice over them with the cream and season again.

Sides: Noodles, dumplings, or sliced potatoes.
You can also cook the potatoes in the pot in coarse pieces.

Roast Wild Duck

For four people		
1–2		wild ducks (depending on size, preferably two smaller ones)
¼	lb.	bacon slices
2		onions
6–8		juniper berries
2	leaves	sage
		sour cream or red wine
		pepper and salt
		fat
		flour to thicken the sauce

Wild ducks are best from August to the end of January. Make very sure that the wax duct on the tail is removed; otherwise the duck will taste oily.

Rub the ducks inside with salt, ground onions, pressed juniper berries and sage. Then brush with fat and cover the thighs and breast with bacon slices. Now fasten the thighs and wings to the body. You can use string or small wooden or metal pins. Now put them in the Dutch oven.

First brown the ducks well on the beast side, then add some water or red wine and cook approx. 90 minutes covered, with upper heat. From time to time pour roasting juice over the ducks.

At the end of the cooking time take the Dutch oven off the coals—also remove the hot coals from the lid—and let the meat set about 15 minutes in the hot pot. Flavor the sauce with red wine or sour cream and bind with some flour.

Sides: Red cabbage and potatoes are classic. When cooking in a Dutch oven, you can add foil-wrapped potatoes to the ducks; they cook very well in the heat beside the pot. You can prepare the red cabbage in a second, smaller Dutch oven. To save coals and space, simply put it on the lid of the "duck pot."

Duck on a Bed of Savoy Cabbage

Duck and Savoy go well together – like goose and red cabbage. For a 14 Dutch Oven.		
2		ducks
½	lb.	bacon
1		large Savoy head (approx. 2½ lbs.)
2		carrots
2		onions
		nutmeg
		clarified butter
		sour cream
		pepper and salt

Remove the legs of the ready-to-cook ducks up to their thighs and quarter them, making eight pieces, each one with a leg or wing standing up. Season the duck pieces with salt and pepper, lay them in melted, clarified butter and cook approx. 1/2 hour with upper and lower heat.

Meanwhile, prepare the Savoy cabbage. Remove outer leaves and stalks and cut into strips. Brown the carrots, cut into discs, and the Savoy briefly in salt water. If you want to prepare the ducks outdoors, you can do these things at home in advance.

Take the duck pieces from the Dutch oven and keep them warm. Now brown the onion rings and bacon pieces in the Dutch oven. Add the Savoy and carrots, season with salt, pepper, and a good pinch of nutmeg, put the duck pieces on it, and cook barely 30 minutes in a closed pot with little upper or lower heat.

A lot of fat is produced; it can be poured or ladled off before serving. Also before serving, put a little cream on the vegetables.

Sides: Baked potato and a nice dry white wine.

Goose on Red Cabbage

This recipe is superbly suitable for preparing a goose with several thousand flight hours. These birds are naturally somewhat fattier, which also does the red cabbage good. This recipe is also very easy to prepare.

For four people and a 14 Dutch Oven		
1		wild or domestic goose (choose size to fit Dutch Oven)
1	cup	bacon cubes
1	cup	onion cubes
		some fat
2	cans	red cabbage
1		somewhat sour apple
		clove powder or cloves (with powder one does not bite the clove, which tastes very unpleasant)
		rosemary
		some juniper berries
		pepper and salt

First cook out the bacon for fat and then steam the onion cubes until glassy. Add the red cabbage and the apple, having cut the latter into small pieces, season with rosemary, juniper, cloves, pepper, and salt, and simmer it all with a few coals under the pot.

Meanwhile turn the lid over, put it on a trivet and heat it with coals. Heat a lot of fat and brown the peppered and salted goose in it. If the goose is too high to fit into the Dutch oven, cut out the back right and left of the spine and break the wishbone in the neck.

When the goose has taken on a good color all around, put it on the red cabbage with breast upward. Now cook the goose and red cabbage together for at least two hours. The fat that cooks out of the goose gives the red cabbage its inimitable flavor.

If there is space in the pot, add potato slices half an hour before the end of the cooking time. Thus, you get a complete meal out of one pot!

Chicken Breast with Mushrooms

A simple dish for a 10 Dutch Oven		
3		chicken breasts with bones
½	lb.	mushrooms, fresh chanterelles or 1 can of Champignons
½	lb.	bacon cubes
2		onions
		pepper and salt
		fat for frying

First salt and pepper the chicken breasts with bones and skin, and brown well in hot fat in the lid with the skin-side down. Then turn the skin-side upward and place the breasts in the Dutch oven.

Brown the cubed onions and bacon and then put them in the pot. Stuff with a can of champignons or—very good—fresh, browned chanterelles, cover and cook half an hour. The chicken breasts are done when the meat can easily be loosened from the bone with a fork.

If you use fresh mushrooms, you must brown them extra in hot fat in the lid—only then will their full aroma develop.

Chicken Breast with Cream Sauce

For a 12 Dutch Oven

10–12		chicken breast fillets	½	tsp.	salt
1	lb.	fresh champignon mushrooms	1	tsp.	curry
1	lb.	onion	1	tsp.	paprika powder
2	cups	cream			pepper and salt
2	cups	sour cream			clarified butter

Brown the chicken breasts without skin (or pork cutlets or turkey breasts) gradually in the lid of the Dutch oven. At the same time, brown the sliced onions and the washed and sliced mushrooms in the Dutch oven. When all the breasts are done, put them in the Dutch oven and salt and pepper them.

Stir the cream and sour cream in a big bowl with the remaining herbs. Pour this over the chicken breasts and put the Dutch oven on the coals, the first hour with only a few coals (six to eight) below, until the meat is soft. Then brown the breasts 1/2 hour to 1 hour with plenty of upper heat (18 to 20 coals).

Sides: Rice or bread, a light summer wine or rosé to drink, and of course beer will also do.

1. Brown the breasts in the lid.

2. Add them to the browned onions and mushrooms in the Dutch oven.

3. The finished dish.

Coq au Vin

This recipe is a must for fans of French cooking. It requires much time, good wine, and a good chicken.

For four people		
2		small chickens (approx. 2lbs. each) or one big spring chicken weighing almost 4lbs.
5		carrots
5		onions
½	lb.	champignon mushrooms, fresh or frozen
¼	lb.	rib bacon
1	bottle	Beaujolais
1	glass	brandy
		flour
		clarified butter
1	sprig	thyme
1		laurel leaf
		pepper and salt

Cut the chickens into portions and remove the skin. Wash the meat and pat dry.

Bring the wine to a boil in the open Dutch oven and reduce it to half. Meanwhile, season the meat with salt and pepper and roll it in flour. Heat clarified butter in the lid of the Dutch oven, brown the meat all around, and put it in the Dutch oven.

Slowly brown the cubed bacon, cubed carrots and coarsely cubed onions in the lid over low heat, and put them in the Dutch oven. Add herbs and brandy, close the lid and stew for an hour. The trick for this dish is to stew as long and at as low a temperature as possible.

After cooking the chicken, brown the fresh mushrooms in clarified butter in the lid and put them in the pot, stew them and the rest for five minutes. Then the dish can be served.

Sides: Baguettes and the wine that was used in cooking.

Chicken Wings

For eight people as an appetizer

4	lbs.	chicken wings
½	cup	olive oil
20–40		whole unpeeled garlic cloves (to taste)

½	tsp.	salt
½	tsp.	pepper
½	tsp.	rosemary
½	tsp.	thyme
½	tsp.	oregano

Layer the chicken wings closely at the bottom of a Dutch oven. Mix the other ingredients in a bowl and pour over the chicken wings. Cover and roast at least an hour. Ideal as appetizers, along with fresh bread dipped in the olive oil-garlic mixture.

Garlic Chicken

A RECIPE FOR GARLIC FANS! For four people and a 14 Dutch Oven.

1		spring chicken of approx. 4lbs.
2–4	heads	garlic (really!)
		olive oil
1	cup	white wine

pepper and salt
cayenne pepper
fresh Provence herbs (rosemary, thyme, etc.)

Divide the chicken into portions, wash, pat dry, brush with olive oil, and season with salt, pepper, and cayenne pepper. Brown to a golden brown all around in an oiled Dutch oven with much heat. Add the unpeeled garlic cloves and herbs, fill with wine and stew with closed lid until the meat falls from the bones.

Remove the garlic from the bowl before eating and rub them on toasted white bread. The separated chicken meat goes on top of them.

Casseroles and Stews

Gunman Stew

A hearty hunter's dinner from a 12 Dutch Oven

2	lbs.	cubed beef	5		medium celery stalks
½	lb.	rib bacon	2		onions
1	lb.	carrots	1	can	peeled tomatoes
2	lbs.	potatoes	½	cup	Worcestershire sauce
2		green peppers, cut small			Tabasco
					pepper and salt
1	cup	soy sauce			oil for frying

First heat the oil in the Dutch oven, then brown the meat in it, and remove it. Next brown the rib bacon and onions. Add the meat again and brown it well. Now add the rest of the ingredients and cook until the vegetables are tender. Season and serve.

This dish can be prepared on a morning in hunting season and cooled at the campfire. In the evening one need only warm up the food.

1. Brown the beef.

2. Add the vegetables.

3. The vegetables are soft after an hour.

4. Now it can be eaten!

BRUNSWICK STEW

For four to six people		
1	lb.	beef
1	lb.	pork
1	lb.	potatoes
1	can	peeled tomatoes
5		onions
3		red peppers
2	tsp.	paprika powder (sweet or sharp, according to taste)
1	tsp.	cumin (whole grains or ground)
1	tsp.	thyme
¼	tsp.	marjoram
½	tsp.	green peppercorns
3–4		juniper berries
		pepper and salt
1		bouillon cube
1	can	champignon mushrooms
		oil
1	squirt	red wine
8	cups	water

Cut the meat into equal-sized cubes and brown it in oil. Season with salt, pepper, green peppercorns, paprika powder, cumin, thyme, and marjoram.

Add small-cut peppers, onion rings, tomatoes, juniper berries and bouillon cube. Sautee this, stirring steadily, fill with water, and simmer approx. 45 minutes. Finally, add the mushrooms and flavor with a squirt of red wine.

Pound Pot

This dish exists in many variations but has a great advantage over the other goulash foods: The meat is not browned. Rather, all ingredients are layered in a pot and then cooked.

For ten people and a 14 or deep 12 Dutch Oven

1	lb.	smoked pork chops	3		paprika peppers
1	lb.	chopped meat	3	cups	cream
1	lb.	beef goulash (false fillet will do)	1	bottle	chili sauce
1	lb.	pork schnitzel	2	tsp.	paprika powder
1	lb.	onions			garlic to taste
1		large can tomatoes			pepper and salt

Cut all ingredients small and put in the pot (the tomatoes with the juice from the can). Make cherry-sized balls of chopped meat and put in the Dutch oven. Then add the chili sauce, cream, and spices, and mix everything carefully.

Heat first with several coals under the pot and cook further with much upper heat (so nothing scorches). The dish thus takes on a second load of coals. When the first load burns out, the food has spent some three hours in the pot and the meat is as soft as the meatballs. You may want to add some fluid at some time.

Sides: Homemade bread or rice.

1. Put all ingredients in the pot.
2. Heat the pot for three hours.
3. A tasty party food with little effort.

Spicy Beef

For six people or a 12 Dutch Oven

2	lbs.	ground beef
4		large onions
1	pack	goulash soup from a bag
1	tbsp.	tomato paste

6	large cucumbers
	Sambal Oelek to taste
	fat for frying
	pepper and salt

Steam the finely cut onions in the Dutch oven until glassy, add the ground beef, and brown it. Add the cubed cucumbers and the tomato paste, sprinkle on the soup powder and fill with 4 cups of water. Season with the spices, add cucumber juice if needed, and cook approx. one hour over low heat.

Sides: Fresh bread or rice.

Hearty Venison Soup

An absolute must for every hunter with at least a 12 or a deep 14 Dutch Oven

	Deer bones
	Deer neck and ribs
3	onions, quartered
1	small celery stalk, cubed
1	leek stem, cut in rings
3	carrots, cut into pieces

¾	lb.	rib bacon, cut in large cubes
1	cup	clarified butter
1	tube	tomato paste
2		laurel leaves
		pepper and salt
		juniper or garlic to taste

This recipe calls for deer bones, which are naturally only to be had if you save them when butchering. In the bone is the marrow, which contains much fat and flavor, which we have omitted in this recipe.

The process is very simple: Cut off the "lower arm" and "lower thigh" with the meat on them by hitting them with the back (important!) of a heavy knife or kitchen cleaver. This is surprisingly easy and is quicker than sawing.

Also save the removed backbones and the bones from the thighs and blades. The ribs are not removed, but only cut apart in twos or threes. The neck remains as it is.

First put half the clarified butter, the bacon cubes, and cubed vegetables in the Dutch oven (or the roaster of an oven), then the bones and meat, and the rest of the vegetables over them, with the rest of the clarified butter. Heat the pot with as many coals on the lid as possible. After a quarter hour, look to see if the ends of the meat are already charred. Now and then move the meat layers so they brown evenly.

When the pieces are brown, carefully pour water into the pot (half a bottle of red wine is not bad either), and cook at least two hours, better three, refilling evaporated water.

When the pieces are so soft that the meat falls off the bones, sieve the soup into another pot with a cloth. This is absolutely necessary because of the splintered bones. The bones are removed and the small-cut meat is put back as a soup ingredient.

Separately cooked noodles, rice, custard, small-cut carrots, peppers, or leeks are suitable ingredients.

If you like, you can also spoon the broth onto a plate and eat the meat along with it.

Season the soup with salt and pepper just before serving. Not much more is necessary.

Bake-Off

Bake-off was formerly a poor people's food from Alsace. This dish was prepared by housewives on wash day and baked three to four hours in a covered baking pan in the baker's oven. Thus, it is very well suited for a large Dutch oven.

For a 14 Dutch Oven

1½	lbs.	pork shoulder
1½	lbs.	beef brisket
1½	lbs.	lamb shoulder without bones, plus pork leg and a pigtail (if you want)
3		large onions
2		leek stems
5		garlic cloves

2		laurel leaves
2		cloves, crushed
3¼	lbs.	potatoes
1	bottle	Alsatian Riesling wine
		pepper and salt
1	tsp.	thyme
1	tsp.	marjoram
		some rosemary

Cut the meat into bite-sized cubes, cut deeply into the pork leg and pigtail at several places, and salt and pepper them. Make a marinade of the wine, the fine-cut garlic cloves, the laurel leaf, cloves, thyme, marjoram, and rosemary sprig. Marinate the meat in it for a day, but not in a Dutch oven, which would rust.

On the following day, peel and slice the potatoes. Make a layer of potato slices, and some leek and onions in the Dutch oven. Cover it with the meat, pork leg, and the rest of the fine-cut onions. Put the rest of the potato slices and onions on the meat. Pour the wine and the rest of the marinade over it. If need be, add some water until the Dutch oven is ¾ full.

Now cook it all at very low heat (about 180 degrees) at least 2½ hours, better 3½ to 4 hours.

Autumn Goulash

For four people		
1	lb.	goulash meat (half beef, half pork)
½	lb.	onions
½	lb.	baking plums
½	lb.	apples
1	cup	meat broth (bouillon cube)
1	cup	cider (sweet)
1	cup	sour or fresh cream
		pepper and salt
		oregano
		oil

The plums must be prepared and soaked in water overnight. Brown the cubed meat well in oil in the Dutch oven and season. Add the onion rings and brown them.

Then fill with broth and cider and put on the coals to stew. After approx. 30 minutes, add the plums, then the sliced apples in another 15 minutes. Let it stew another 15 minutes.

The sour cream is stirred in before serving, making the dish nice and smooth.

Sides: Dumplings (from a package).

Wild Boar and Bean Soup

When butchering a wild boar, good pieces of meat are left that are very small and not worth freezing. These bits of meat are sorted out at once and gathered in a bowl.

Just right for a wild boar butchering festival		
2	lbs.	wild boar meat, cut small (beef or any other meat will do)
3		carrots
3		onions
5		tomatoes
1		large can red kidney beans
1		large can white beans, cooked with soup cabbage
		pepper and salt
½	tsp.	cross cumin
½	tsp.	sweet paprika
½	tsp.	cayenne pepper
		plenty of Marjoram (it goes very well with wild boar)
		clarified butter for frying

Heat a tablespoon of clarified butter strongly in the Dutch oven and brown the meat very much in portions of all sizes. The browning is responsible for the color of the complete soup.

Add the chopped onions to the browned meat and brown them. When the onions are a golden yellow, add the cut-up carrots and small-cut tomatoes. Brown briefly and then fill with the drained red beans and not-drained white beans. Fill one of the empty cans with water and add it to the pot.

Season the soup very strongly with much pepper, salt, cayenne, paprika, cumin, and marjoram, and cook for two hours until it attains a creamy consistency. Thus cooked, the soup is midway between soup and stew.

As you wish, eat it with potatoes or from the soup bowl on a slice of bread.

Turnip Casserole

For four people		
1	lb.	diced turkey
1		small turnip, about 2 lbs.
3		onions
		oil or clarified butter
3	cups	broth
1	cup	sour cream
		pepper and salt
		curry (sweet)
		sugar
		parsley
		lemon juice

Brown the meat in clarified butter and season with salt, pepper and curry. Add the cubed onions, brown, fill with broth and stew about half an hour. Then add the cubed turnip. Let it simmer about an hour and a half until the turnips are soft.

Stir in the sour cream and, if you want, add a little curry and a squirt of lemon juice, for the turnips will take up some of the spices. Simmer five minutes, then serve.

Before serving, scatter chopped parsley over the casserole.

Sides: white or pita bread.

SPICY BEAN CASSEROLE

For ten people and a deep 12 or 14 Dutch Oven		
2	lbs.	chopped meat
2	lbs.	onions
1		big can white beans
1		big can red kidney beans
2		small cans chili beans
2		large cans peeled tomatoes
1		large jar red pepper strips, sour
2	tsp.	sweet paprika
2	tsp.	salt
2	tsp.	ground pepper
		Oil
		Chili powder to taste
		Bouillon cube or broth from a jar for 2 liters of fluid

Brown the chopped meat in olive oil and crumble it, take it out of the Dutch oven, and brown the chopped onions in fresh olive oil. Put the browned meat back in the pot.

Cut up the tomatoes thoroughly in the can with a long knife and put them in the Dutch oven. Dissolve the bouillon cube in the remaining juice and put it in the Dutch oven. Then add the sour-packed peppers (with juice) and the other beans (also with juice), season with the spices, and cook at least half an hour.

Spicy bean casserole.

For this casserole, homemade bread and cold beer are simply a must.

Cheese Soup (also called Cheeseburger Soup)

For a deep 12 or a 14 Dutch Oven		
2	lbs.	chopped meat
2	packs	cream cheese, each 7 oz. or 14 tbsp.
1		large can champignon mushrooms
6	stems	leek
4		onions
2	cups	fresh cream
12	cups	broth
		oil
		chili powder
		sweet paprika
		some nutmeg
		pepper and salt

Brown the chopped meat in oil in the Dutch oven, crumble fine, and take out of the Dutch oven. Brown the onions (cut into rings), leek, and mushrooms in the Dutch oven, add the browned meat, fill with broth, and simmer briefly.

Then stir in fresh cream and let the cheese melt slowly in small pieces. Season with the spices and serve.

You can also prepare the soup, let it cool, and warm it up before serving.

But be careful with this soup at summer parties, as it starts to get done very quickly in humid weather, especially in large quantities, which need a long time to cool. Goulash soups are better here.

GOULASH

Goulash is a subject in itself. There are countless recipes, and each claims to be the right one. Do not let yourself be confused by goulash. It is first of all a casserole in which whatever is at hand is cooked—and that is how you should regard goulash. It is possible to make goulash a little thinner as a soup, for which the meat must be cut in cherry-sized pieces. As a meat added to dumplings or noodles, the meat goes better in plum-sized chunks.

For four to six people and a 12 Dutch Oven		
2	lbs.	goulash meat, half and half
½	lb.	smoked bacon cubes
1	can	peeled tomatoes, 2 cups
5		onions
1		each red, green, and yellow peppers
1	tsp.	each thyme, cumin, marjoram, ground pepper
2	tsp.	sweet paprika
1	tsp.	salt
1	tsp.	seasoning salt
1	can	chanterelle mushrooms

Brown the meat well on all sides in the Dutch oven or in the lid, add the spices, then brown the coarsely chopped onions until they are glassy. Add the pepper pieces and sautee lightly.

Put the peeled tomatoes in the pot and fill with liquid, 8 cups of water, or, even better, broth.

Close the lid and simmer two hours with six to ten coals below. For this dish it does not matter if the pot cools because the coals have burned out. One can also let the pot simmer in a dying campfire before one, for example, goes hunting.

Before serving, brown the mushrooms on the upside-down lid. This is necessary because the mushrooms only form or release their aromas when they are heated over 100 degrees in hot fat. Without this treatment, the mushrooms remain without their usual taste, and their use would be a waste of money.

Then, add the browned mushrooms and season the goulash with pepper and salt.

1. The ingredients are browned in the Dutch oven.

2. You can also brown the meat in the lid.

3. You must brown the mushrooms in the lid, for the pot is full.

4. A nice goulash with tender meat and many colorful vegetables.

Potatoes with Meatballs

For a 14 Dutch Oven

1	lb.	potatoes
1	pack	frozen buttered or stir-fried vegetables
1	cup	cream
1	cup	sour cream
1	tbsp.	mustard
1	tsp.	sugar
		pepper and salt

For the meat balls:

1	lb.	chopped meat, half and half
1		onion
1		raw egg
1		stale bread, softened in water and squeezed out
		garlic powder or fresh garlic, to taste
		pepper and salt

Distribute the cooked potato slices evenly in the Dutch oven.

Make a dough of the ground meat, the raw egg, the finely chopped onion, the garlic, and the roll, and season with salt and pepper. Make cherry-sized balls and place evenly on the potato slices. Distribute the frozen vegetables evenly between them.

Mix the cream, sour cream, mustard, and sugar, and season with pepper and salt. Put this material over the ingredients in the Dutch oven. With a few coals under the oven and more on the lid, roast approx. 45 minutes until the upper parts of the meat balls become brown.

Pepper Soup

The right thirst-maker for a men's evening with ten people, for a 14 Dutch oven.

3	lbs.	chopped meat
2	lbs.	onions
6		cabanossi sausage
5	stalks	leek
2		large cans kidney beans
1		small tube tomato paste
		oil for frying
8	cups	broth (can be from bouillon cubes)
1	can	green peppers
2	tsp.	mustard
		salt, cayenne pepper, or chili powder

Brown the chopped meat in the Dutch oven and crumble it, take it out of the pot to brown the cubed onions and the leek, cut into small rings.

Add the tomato paste, the chopped meat, and the cabanossi, cut into finger-size slices, to the pot, and fill with broth.

Put the beans and the dried green peppers in the pot. Season with mustard, salt, cayenne pepper or chili powder, and cook 20 minutes. If need be, bind the mixture with potato flour or cornstarch.

PEAS, SAUSAGE, AND FAT MEAT

This recipe produces a nourishing soup.

For two people		
1	can	pureed peas
1	can	SPAM
1	cup	bacon cubes
1	cup	onion cubes

Put the pureed peas and the balls of SPAM (potted meat) in the Dutch oven, fill with exactly the specified 6 1/3 cups of water and boil. Or put the can of pureed peas in the Dutch oven and dilute it with water to make a thick fluid soup.

Spread out the bacon on the upside-down lid and brown the onions along with the bacon. Pour them over the soup and serve. If you want, a few Vienna sausages can be cut into slices and warmed up in the soup.

Corned Beef

For two people		
1		large can sauerkraut
3		onions
1	can	corned beef
2		cabanossi sausage, cut into slices
1	lb.	potatoes
		beer
		pepper and salt, cumin to taste

Layer the sauerkraut, potato slices cooked like bacon, plucked beef, sausage slices, and onion rings in a Dutch oven alternately. Pepper and salt richly, add cumin if you like it, and pour beer on it.

After an hour, a simple but filling bachelor meal is finished!

Hearty Casserole

For eight to ten people and a 12 Dutch Oven		
1	lb.	each beef, pork, and lamb meat
3	cups	chicken and beef broth
1		large can peeled tomatoes
9	cups	fresh cubed vegetables, your choice
2	cups	frozen peas
1	can	kidney beans
⅓	cup	flour
⅔	cup	cold water
		oil
		basil
		oregano
2		laurel leaves
		Worcestershire sauce to taste
		pepper and salt

Heat the oil in the Dutch oven and brown the meat cubes. Take the excess fat out of the pot and pour the tomatoes and broth over the meat. Add the spices and then the Worcestershire sauce.

Bring this to a boil and then mix in the vegetables. Boil again and then simmer approx. 20 minutes.

Add the frozen peas and boil again until the peas are soft. Mix the flour and water and then add it to the food to thicken it. Season it with salt and pepper and serve.

Diced Meat with Green Beans

For a 10 or 12 Dutch Oven		
2	lbs.	cutlet meat (pork or turkey)
2	lbs.	fresh green beans
		fresh bean cabbage
½	lb.	fresh champignon mushrooms
4		onions
2	cups	sour cream
4	cups	broth
		pepper and salt
		oil
		some flour

Brown the onions and the mushrooms, cut these into fine slices, in oil in the Dutch oven, add the cut beans and steam briefly. Then pour on the broth, put the bean cabbage on the beans, and cook lightly for 20 minutes over low heat. Then remove the bean cabbage and throw it away.

Now take off the lid and place it upside-down on the lid base. Put the coals under it and brown the meat on the lid. Mix the browned meat into the beans, pour on the two containers of sour cream, and cook another 30 minutes.

Feta-Potato Casserole

For a 12 Dutch Oven		
2	lbs.	potatoes
7	oz.	feta cheese
2		onions
½	lb.	cooked ham
1	cup	cream
1	cup	fresh cream
		pepper and salt
		paprika, nutmeg
		parsley
2		eggs
		oil or butter

Cut up the onions and steam in the Dutch oven until glassy. Cut the ham small and brown with them briefly, then remove from the pot. Crumble the feta, wash, and peel the potatoes and cut into thin slices. Mix the cream, fresh cream, eggs, and spices in a bowl with a fork.

Layer the potatoes, feta, and onion-ham mixture in the Dutch oven and pour the sauce over it.

Bake in the Dutch oven for 40 to 60 minutes. If you like cheese, you can scatter ground Swiss cheese over the casserole at the end of the cooking time and gratinize it with high upper heat.

Spanish Fricco

For a 12 Dutch Oven		
2	lbs.	red potatoes
½	lb.	beef or pork
½	lb.	onions
1	tbsp.	butter
1	cup	cream
¼	cup	hot water
		Pepper and salt, plus Provence vegetables if you want

Grease the Dutch oven with the butter, then put in the thin slices of potato, the cubed meat, and the onion rings in layers. Season each layer with salt and pepper plus spices. Make several layers in the pot and cover with the potatoes.

Cook at least two hours over low heat, longer does no harm.

Serve this dish with cucumbers.

SOLJANKA

The Russian occupation troops in Germany after World War II left behind a great dish: Soljanka. It is actually a typical leftover meal, so the ingredients vary depending on what is available. But the cucumbers are vital, for they give the dish its typical acidic taste.

For a 12 Dutch Oven

2	beef leg pieces
2	pork neck cutlets
2	cabanossi (or other cold-cut leftovers such as mortadella)
4	onions
2	carrots
1	jar tomato paprika (sour preserves)
4	large cucumbers
5	pimento seeds
	pepper and salt
	paprika
	clarified butter
	sour cream for serving

Brown the meat (it can also be roast leftovers) in clarified butter in the Dutch oven, fill with eight cups of water and cook an hour, until the meat loosens from the bones. Take the meat off the bones and cut into small cubes. Pour the broth out of the Dutch oven and keep it.

Brown the not too finely cut slices of onion, carrot, dried tomato paprika and cucumbers in clarified butter in the Dutch oven. Then add the meat and the finely sliced cold cuts and pour on the meat broth.

Cook with a few coals for at least two hours, until the vegetables are soft. Season with salt, pepper, paprika powder, and five pimento seeds, perhaps also with some cucumber water, since the Soljanka should have a piquant acidic taste. Put a scoop of sour cream on each plate when serving.

Soljanka tastes even better when warmed up!

Side: White bread.

TIP!

In any case, you should take the Soljanka out of the Dutch oven as quickly as possible. The acidic content very quickly makes the Dutch oven rust.

Spicy Sauerkraut Soup

For at least a 12 Dutch Oven, but bigger is better		
2	lbs.	sauerkraut or two big cans
5		onions
½	lb.	bacon
10		bratwurst or 1½ lbs. chopped meat
1	can	peeled tomatoes
5	quarts	broth from bouillon cubes
		oil
		paprika powder
		pepper and salt
		Sambal Oelek
		sugar

Brown the sauerkraut in a little oil in the Dutch oven, fill with the broth and the liquid from the tomatoes, and boil.

Brown the cut-up onions and cubed bacon in portions in the lid of the Dutch oven and add to the sauerkraut. Press the stuffing out of the bratwurst in the form of small balls and brown them. Or make small balls of the seasoned chopped meat and add them to the sauerkraut when browned.

Season with salt, pepper, Sambal Oelek, and sugar. Cook 1/2 hour at moderate temperature. Then add the tomato pieces and stir, then bring to a boil again.

Pea Soup

For a reasonable pea soup, you need time plus the eight ingredients. But then it is unbeatable for awakening frozen forms out by a campfire in winter.

For six to eight people		
1½	lbs.	dried peas, soaked overnight
2	lbs.	Schweinenacken or smoked pork chops
½	lb.	rib bacon
5		onions
5	stalks	leek
1		large celery stalk
		pepper and salt
		fat for frying

Heat the fat in the Dutch oven and then brown the cubed bacon along with the cubed onions.

Then add the leek, cut into rings, the cubed celery and meat, and the peas with the soaking water, filling the whole thing with water if needed.

The soup must cook at least an hour—two hours don't hurt. Season with salt and pepper and cook another quarter hour.

TIP!

A good pea soup can be eaten with a fork!

TIP!

The soup is even tastier if a pig's foot is cooked along with it.

TIP!

Season the soup with strong mustard!

Lentils with Noodles

For four people		
1½	lbs.	lentils, soaked overnight, or two large cans
2	lbs.	sausage
½	lb.	rib bacon
2		onions
4	stalks	leek
1		large celery stalk
		some celery greens
1	lb.	noodles
1		large tube tomato paste
2		laurel leaves
		pepper and salt
		fat for frying

Cook the noodles in salt water in the Dutch oven as directed, let drip dry and put aside.

Brown the cubed bacon and onions in the Dutch oven, add the rings of leek and the cubed celery, and steam them.

Then add the lentils with the soaking water and bring to a boil. Season with salt and pepper and cook for an hour. Add the small-cut sausage and cook another quarter hour.

Mix the noodles and tomato paste in a bowl and then add to the lentil dish, stir briefly, and boil again, so the noodles get hot again.

You can flavor the dish with a squirt of vinegar if you wish.

BEANS

Baked Beans and Ham

For about ten people and a 12 Dutch Oven		
2	lbs.	ham, cubed
2	lbs.	red beans, soaked the previous day, or 4 large cans
4		onions
1	cup	tomato ketchup (or 1 can tomato paste)
½	cup	brown sugar
1	tbsp.	medium sharp mustard

Brown the onions in some oil in the Dutch oven. Add the other ingredients and bake for some 2 1/2 hours with coals above and below the Dutch oven. Take off the lid for the last half hour, so the moisture can evaporate. Then put the lid on for ten minutes and put on as many coals as will fit.

COWBOY BEANS

For six to eight people (counted as a side dish) and a 10 Dutch Oven		
3	cups	bacon
3	cups	onions
1		large can kidney beans
½	cup	chili sauce
½	cup	tomato paste
2	tsp.	mustard
1	tbsp.	sugar
		pepper and salt
		Sambal Oelek
		butter or olive oil

Cook down the bacon cubes in a goodly amount of butter or olive oil in the Dutch oven. Add the cubed onions and steam with the bacon until glassy. Fill the pot with kidney beans and close the lid.

That was the contents, or better, the substance. Now comes the flavor! It must be spicy. But how? Best with a chili sauce. But that generally doesn't do the job alone, so add pepper, salt, mustard, Sambal Oelek, and tomato paste. For dishes of this kind, the sweet note is often forgotten; they are spicy but taste somewhat weak. So add some sugar or sweet ketchup.

Put the coals on the lid to produce upper heat. The pot, fully seasoned, must cook on the fire for a time.

I make this dish as a side for grilled meat and thus put the Dutch oven on the grill. Then a handful of coals suffice to bring the pot to a boil and stay warm one or two hours. One has a hard time waiting!

Such dishes taste best when they are cooked and then warmed up.

Chili con Carne

The standard dish for the Dutch Oven, for four people.		
1	lb.	chopped meat
2	cups	strained tomatoes
2		red peppers
2		large onions
1	can	corn
2		large cans kidney beans
1	pack	chili spice mixture
		pepper and salt
		oil
1	tbsp.	sugar, or some sweet ketchup
		maybe Tabasco

First brown the chopped meat with the onions. Brown the crumbled meat thoroughly in oil in the Dutch oven. Then add the onion and pepper cubes and let them become glassy. Now add salt and pepper, to taste.

Add the strained tomatoes and the drip-dried beans and let it all soak approx. 30 minutes with light upper and lower heat. If need be, add water or broth if the material is too dry. Now add the sugar or ketchup and cook another ten minutes.

Shortly before the end of the cooking time, season again and add the corn, but just let it get hot, so it remains chewy.

Chili in XXL

The 20-man portion for the deep 14 Dutch Oven		
2	lbs.	chopped meat
2	lbs.	onions
2	lbs.	cubed bacon
2	cans	kidney beans, 5 quarts each
2		large cans corn (2 cups)
2	tubes	tomato paste
2	bottles	chili sauce
		olive oil
		pepper and salt
		chili powder

Brown the chopped meat in individual portions in the Dutch oven and take it out of the pot. Then brown the cubed onions until glassy, take them out of the pot and brown the bacon. When the bacon is glassy, put the chopped meat and onions back in the pot.

Pour off about 1/4 of the fluid from the bean cans and put the beans in the Dutch oven. Add the tomato paste and chili sauce, season with pepper, salt, and much chili, and simmer for an hour. Add the corn and simmer 15 minutes more, so the corn is still chewy. Season again, maybe with seasoning salt, and serve.

Serbian Bean Soup

For a 14 Dutch Oven		
2	lbs.	dried white beans, soaked overnight
2	lbs.	potatoes
1	lb.	rib bacon
4		carrots
4		leek stems
½	stalk	celery
		celery greens
5		big onions
1		large tube tomato paste
2	tsp.	marjoram
2	tsp.	sweet paprika
4		cabanossi sausage
1	cup	sour cream
		pepper and salt
		fat for frying

Heat the fat in a Dutch oven and cook out the cubed bacon. Steam the cubed onions and the potatoes in the fat, then add the small-cut carrots, the leek stems cut in rings, and the small-cut celery, and steam them. Add the beans in their soaking water, the tomato paste, and the spices.

First put all the coals under the pot and cook the soup strongly for five minutes, then simmer two hours with little lower heat. Before serving, cook the sliced cabanossi with it for a quarter hour.

Season with pepper, salt, and paprika, and mix in the sour cream.

FISH

A Dutch oven is really not suited for fish, since they need only short cooking times, while the Dutch oven is designed for long, slow simmering (cooking a bit under the boiling point). Yet, you can also bread or fry fish—then the black pots are suitable again.

If you are already out at an open fire, you probably grill the fish and prepare a side dish in the Dutch oven.

For those who would like to see something other than grilled fish on the menu after several weeks in the bush, here are a few recipes.

Baked Trout

Per person		
1		trout
1	tbsp.	butter
		lemon wedges
		pepper and salt
		fresh greens, as available

Melt a good bit of butter in a Dutch oven. Rub the cleaned and gutted trout with salt and pepper inside and out. Add a few herbs to taste, such as fresh dill. Put the trout in the Dutch oven and bake approx. 20 minutes.

Then remove the lid, pour a sauce of melted butter and lemon juice over it, and serve.

Sausage and Shrimp

For four people		
1	lb.	cabanossi sausage
1	lb.	frozen and shelled shrimp
2		onions
4		garlic cloves
2	cups	water
1	can	peeled tomatoes
1	tsp.	thyme
1	tsp.	salt
2	cups	uncooked rice
		olive oil

Brown the sliced cabanossi and the chopped onions in some olive oil in the Dutch oven until the onions turn glassy. Then add the finely chopped garlic. Fill the pot with the can of tomatoes, which should be cut into several pieces in the can with a long knife first. Include the juice and add the two cups of water. Season with salt, pepper, and thyme.

As soon as the soup boils, add the rice and the defrosted shrimp. Cook the whole thing until the rice is done. Add water if needed.

Cajun Style Fish Fillet

For four people		
8–12		fish fillets
2	cups	mustard
3		eggs beaten together
1	tsp.	Tabasco
2	cups	breadcrumbs
2	tsp.	Cajun spice mixture (see page 166)
1	tsp.	garlic powder
1	tsp.	paprika powder
		lemon wedges
1	tsp.	red pepper
1	cup	flour
		olive oil

Heat at least ¾" of olive oil almost to smoking in the bottom of the Dutch oven. The mixed dry ingredients are in the inverted lid as a coating.

Mix the eggs, mustard and Tabasco in a bowl. First turn the fish fillets in the liquid mixture, then in the seasoned breadcrumbs, then fry them five minutes on each side in the Dutch oven.

Before serving, let them drip on a folded kitchen towel. Serve with lemon wedges.

Red Perch with Crackly Crust

For a 10 Dutch Oven		
1	lb.	potatoes
1	pack	spinach
1	lb.	red or gold perch fillet
2	cups	tomatoes (also as a tetra-pack)
		lemon juice
¼	lb.	ground Swiss cheese
1	cup	breadcrumbs
		butter
		pepper and salt

Coat the Dutch oven liberally with butter and lay out the cooked potato slices. Salt and pepper, then spread the spinach on top.

Sprinkle the fish with lemon juice and salt, place on the spinach, and pour the cut-up tomatoes over it. Mix breadcrumbs with the ground cheese and sprinkle over the fish.

Put chips of butter on top and bake about 30 minutes with low upper and lower heat.

This dish also goes well with cooked rice of potato puree instead of the potato slices.

SIDE DISHES

Baked Potatoes

Select a Dutch oven of the right size, cover the bottom with a ¾" thick layer of coarse salt, and press one large or two small potatoes per person into the salt. After three quarters of an hour with upper and lower heat, you can carefully stick a fork into a potato to see if it is done.

The potatoes in a salt bed in a large Dutch oven.

After about an hour the baked potatoes are done.

Dutch Oven Potatoes

Per person and for a 12 Dutch Oven		
1		large potato
½–1		onion
½	lb.	bacon
		shredded cheese (to taste)
		pepper and salt
1	cup	water or broth

Brown the cubed bacon and onions in some oil in the Dutch oven. Then add the potato slices and season well. Other spices, such as hot paprika powder, etc., can also be used according to your taste.

Pour on the cup of water or broth so the potatoes cook first in steam until the liquid evaporates. Put the lid on the Dutch oven and cover with coals. Cook until the potatoes are done (approx. 20 minutes).

Then strew the cheese over the food and wait until it has melted.

Serve the Dutch oven potatoes as hot as you can, whether as a main course or side dish, which is up to you.

Above: The potatoes with bacon and onions in the Dutch oven.
Below: after being baked with cheese.

Potatoes Au Gratin

A good potato au gratin is always a popular side dish, and thanks to prepared sauces, it is also easy to prepare in camp.

Per person		
1		large potato (as a side dish)
½		onion
~*½	cup	cream or, better, prepared gratin sauce
~2	oz.	grated Swiss cheese for gratinizing
		pepper and salt

* ~ = Approximately

Peel the potatoes and onions, combine them in the Dutch oven, salt and pepper, and then pour the sauce over the potatoes. If the sauce does not flow readily, add some water down in the Dutch oven, so the potatoes do not scorch.

Now cook the potatoes, first with lower heat, until they are soft. Then put the cheese over the potatoes and gratinize with upper heat.

A delicious potato au gratin.

Chili Meat Sauce for Baked Potatoes

For a 8 Dutch Oven					
3/4	lb.	chopped meat	2	tbsp.	chili sauce
2		small cans chili beans	1		onion (cubed)
			1		crushed garlic clove
1	cup	water	1	tsp.	Tabasco sauce

Puree the chili beans in a blender. Brown the chopped meat well, along with the cubed onions and garlic from the press, in the Dutch oven. As soon as the onions become glassy, add the rest of the ingredients. Stir briefly and simmer lightly for an hour. This sauce tastes terrific over baked potatoes.

Corn Ears

Corn ears are part of a real American barbecue. Fortunately, they are very easy to prepare.

Per person		
1		fresh corn ear with leaves
1	slice	bacon
		butter and salt

Peel the sweet corn so the leaves stay on. Remove the fine silk from the ear and wrap a slice of bacon around it in spiral form. Then fold the leaves back, wrap with cotton thread or string, and soak the corn for an hour. Then put the corn on the grill for half an hour, or directly on the coals. The soaking lets it take up enough moisture so it will not burn until it is done. When the outer leaves are burned, take the ears from the fire, cut the string and remove the bacon. The corn can then be eaten with butter and salt.

Potatoes in Foil

This side dish is wonderfully suitable for outdoor events. Medium-sized potatoes are wrapped in aluminum foil and simply placed among the coals. Depending on their size, the potatoes need a cooking time of 45 to 60 minutes.

A very tasty variant of the foil potato: Make a hole lengthwise through the potato with an apple corer and fill it with strips of leek. Then wrap the potato in a slice of bacon, cover it with aluminum foil and put it among the coals.

TIP!

The microwave is a great help for pre-cooking potatoes. Simply poke all around the potato with a fork, put it in the microwave, and let it turn for five minutes at 600 watts. Then cut up the potato and either grill it or roast it in the coals.

Potatoes with Cumin

A very simple dish that goes well with grilled food

new potatoes

olive oil

1 mixture of coarse salt and cumin in equal parts

Do not peel the potatoes, but only wash them under flowing water with a crude brush. Then halve them lengthwise; cut a "standing surface" for very round potatoes, so the potato half stands with the big cut surface upward.

Pour olive oil into a saucer and put the salt-cumin mixture in another. First dip the cut surface of the potato in the oil and then in the salt-cumin mixture. Brush the Dutch oven with olive oil and put the potatoes in it with the cut side up. Cook approx. 30 minutes with little lower and much upper heat.

Stuffed Champignons

A piquant side dish for grilled meat, which can also be prepared in a Dutch oven with grilled tomatoes and onions.

large champignon mushrooms	parsley
one small piece of feta cheese per mushroom	olive oil
onion	pepper and salt

Clean the mushrooms with a dry brush and break off the stems, so the hollow heads remain upright.

Chop the onion fine, stir the parsley, olive oil, salt, and pepper into a smooth mass and fill the mushroom heads with it. Set a piece of feta cheese on each head and put them in the Dutch oven, which has been brushed with olive oil. Steam half an hour with low lower and high upper heat.

Grilled Tomatoes

tomatoes	parmesan
garlic	butter
oregano	olive oil
pepper and salt	

Set firm tomatoes on the stem base and cut crosswise at the point with a sharp knife. Pull back the skin. Season with pepper, salt, oregano, and garlic juice, sprinkle with parmesan, and crown with a butter chip.

Put them in the Dutch oven, which has been brushed with olive oil. Steam them half an hour with low lower and high upper heat.

Grilled Onions

onions	Parmesan
olive oil	pepper and salt

Peal the onions, but cut only a little of the root away, and divide lengthwise so they still hang together by the roots.

Dip the cut surface in olive oil, salt and pepper, and sprinkle with Parmesan to taste. Steam them until glassy in a Dutch oven with the cut surfaces up.

Blooming Onions

Per portion		
1	large onion	some butter
1	garlic clove	pepper and salt

Peel the onion, but do not remove the roots completely, but just stroke the dry roots with your fingers. Then cut crosswise into the onion from above, so the onion hangs together by the roots.

Stir a paste of butter, pepper, and salt, and put a teaspoonful of it plus a peeled garlic clove into the onion.

Then lay the onion on a piece of firm aluminum foil and wrap the ends of the foil upward over the onion, attaching them to each other. Bake each bundle about half an hour in the hot glow. After you open the foil, the onion "blooms."

BREAD AND ROLLS

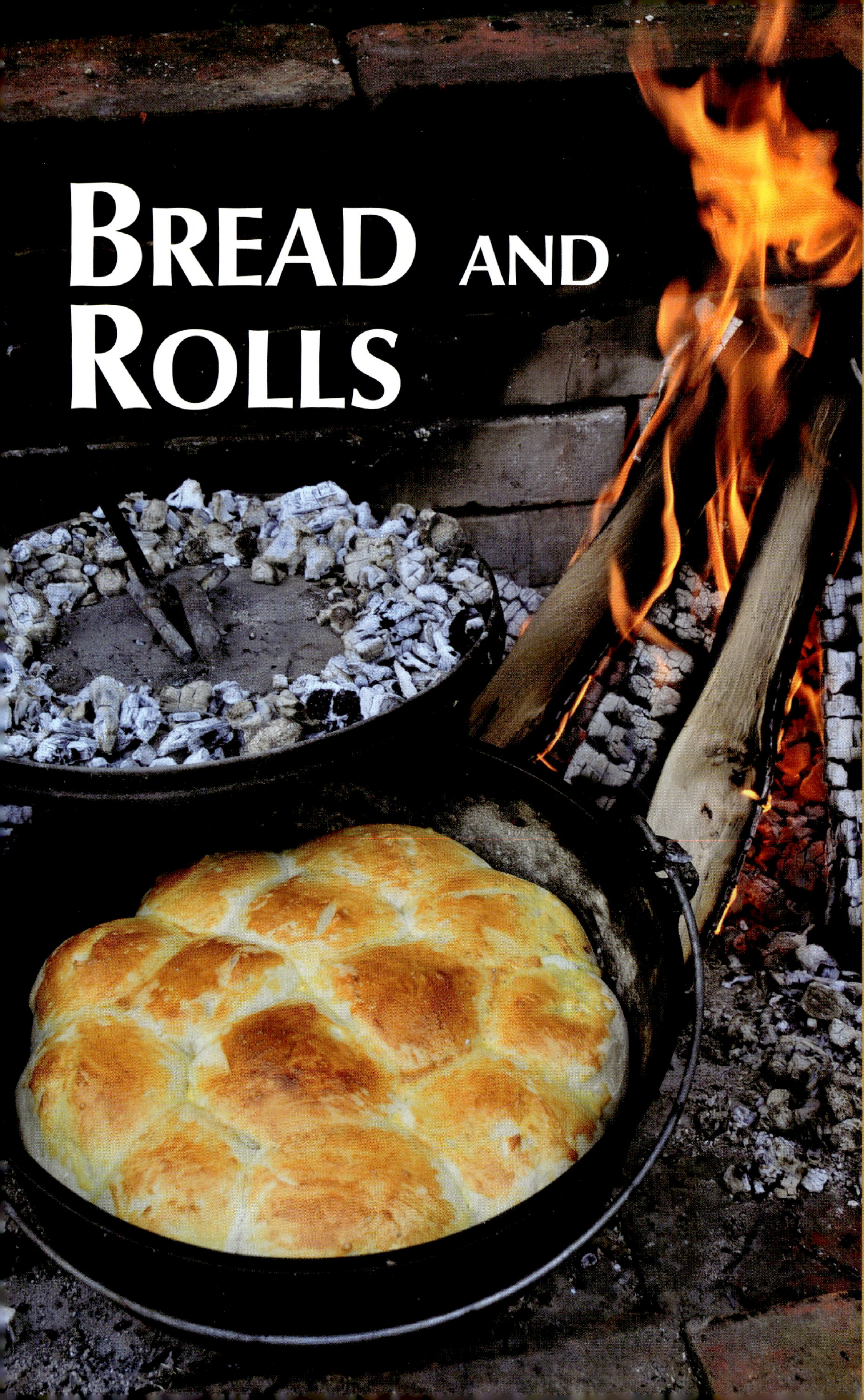

IN GENERAL

In America, the life style of the pioneers caused a very different bread culture to develop. Individual families moved westward in search of farmland and, under Abraham Lincoln's Homestead Act in 1862, could very easily obtain up to 160 acres of land. They only needed to cultivate and improve the land to fulfill a contract—and after a year they owned the land free of cost. So it happened that each of the new citizens lived in a small cabin amid 160 acres of land, and the distance to their nearest neighbor was too long to allow baking bread together. So the settlers baked their own bread in the fireplace, which was at the same time their cooking place. And they usually used a Dutch oven. The number of inhabitants in such a farmhouse was relatively small, usually including only the family, with three or four children. There were no servants.

The housewife baked bread or rolls every day, to be served with warm food. On the cattle drives, "rolls and gravy"—rolls and a sauce of cooked-out bacon and flour—were a common dish.

A woman in pioneer dress bakes at the fireplace.

Baking Over a Campfire

Scarcely anything fascinates people at a campfire as much as someone who is capable of baking something interesting. Anybody can grill, but baking, that is big-league. In cooking courses in particular one sees again and again how difficult baking seems to be. One thing is sure: Whoever has not yet baked, not even at home, has no chance of achieving good results at a campfire. Preparing the dough must work from the start, for baking over an uneven fire requires enough attention.

The Alpha and Omega: The Right Flour

Flour is not simply flour. And using the right flour is decisive in baking bread.

- **Pastry Flour** is a wheat flour, the most often-sold flour in the supermarket. It is suitable only as cooking flour.

- **All-Purpose Flour** is a wheat flour suitable for rolls and white bread, thus for baked goods that are supposed to rise well, or for pizza dough.

- **Rye Flour** is intended for hearty bread. Because of its poor baking qualities it must be either mixed with wheat flour or modified with sourdough.

Leavening Agent: Yeast, Sourdough, or Baking Powder

A dough of water, flour, and salt never becomes a loose bakery product, but an oblate or Jewish matzo. To breathe life into the bread, one needs either yeast, similar living organisms, or baking powder as a chemical agent.

Let us begin with the simplest one, baking powder. Is consists of natron and a leavening agent and breaks down under heat and dampness into, among other things, carbon dioxide, which forms bubbles that lighten the dough. When you work with baking powder, it is important that the dough not be very strongly kneaded or moved after its addition, for once the baking powder is used up, it produces no more bubbles that can raise the dough. Bread made with baking powder always tastes dull and boring; thus, it is more suitable for mixed cake.

Developed yeasts are another leavening agent; they consume the sugar in the dough and give off alcohol as well as carbon dioxide and thus make the dough rise. The best results are achieved at temperatures between 80 and 90 degrees Fahrenheit. The dough is modified with the yeast, kneaded and set aside until it has doubled. Then it is kneaded again, but only a little, so as not to let all the carbon dioxide escape. Now shape rolls and let them go a second time until they have doubled. Then comes the baking, in which the dough rises another time. The yeast gives the dough a typical flavor; thus you should allow time for it to do its work. For yeast dough, wheat flower is always the first choice. You should try yeast dough a few times at home before you set out to bake with it at a campfire.

The Top Class: Sourdough

For the right baking at a campfire, it is best to use sourdough. Everyone knows the expression "greenhorn" refers to a newcomer to the Wild West. The opposite was an "Old Sourdough," who could bake "bannocks" (the favorite kind of rolls among trappers) with sourdough. The sourdough was kneaded with so much flour that it became crumbly. Thus, it did not bake further, but could be wrapped in a cloth and carried in one's pants pocket.

Rye flour in particular requires a sour dough, so that the flour for baking is opened up and a better result comes about. Besides, the sourdough not only improves the baking qualities but also the flavor. Sourdough can be made with either wheat or rye flour. In Germany, sourdough made of rye is customary; Americans incline more to wheat sourdough.

This is how a real bubbly sourdough made of rye should look.

Tips and Tricks:

• In preparing dough, you should strive for the right consistency on the dry side, first making a dry dough and then adding more and more water until it is suitable. Thus, the amount of flour remains constant. If the dough is too liquidy and you add more flour, the yeast-salt-flour ratio is no longer right.

• Wheat flour gets better with kneading; dough made with rye flour does not. Here you can save work.

The lighter the bread, the sooner you're dead.

• Rye flour sticks terribly and was formerly mixed with linseed oil or water as a glue.

• Bowls befouled with rye dough should not be washed, but put in the sun and left to dry; then the dry layer can be knocked off.

• Sourdough bread with yeast has an unpleasant yeasty taste when oven-fresh. It disappears after a day.

Mill-fresh and oven warm, makes the richest farmer poor.

• Rye dough is inclined to contract and become firmer as pancake dough. The pancake dough then becomes tougher and thicker, so that you have to mix water into it again.

• A nice warm place to let dough rise when you are camping is in the car, where interior temperatures over 122 degrees Fahrenheit occur in the sun and the environment is wind-free.

Sourdough

One of the great advantages of the Dutch oven is that one can bake in it with sourdough, which is dough turned sour, a water-flour mixture that is affected by wild yeast fungi of the most varied origins, that occur in the air. The dough makes bubbles and grows, and tastes sour as if in a brewery. Some years ago sourdough called "Hermann" was found on almost every kitchen windowsill; now it has become a secret again.

The simplest way is to get a piece of Hermann from the baker. It is basically given or stolen—as with flower growers—but never paid for. Then it does not grow. And one need not worry about it.

The trick in baking with sourdough is that this leavened dough gives flavor to the baked goods. The power of the wild yeast is modest, so that the dough has to have more and more rising agents such as baking powder or dry yeast mixed into it. A bread made only of flour, water, sugar, and salt, perhaps with baking powder or yeast, always tastes slightly sweet. Only by adding sourdough does the bread become hearty and wholesome, and it stays fresh longer.

To raise sourdough, one must not use any plastic or metal; only glass and stoneware or porcelain are suitable. The bowl is covered—it must not be more than half-full—with a clean kitchen towel. The sourdough should always be in a warm place, and must be used every day, or at least every other day. It lasts better in the refrigerator, where one need only feed it new flour and water once a week. If one uses sourdough for baking, the mass one uses should be replaced by a fresh mixture. The process is very simple: First one takes the sourdough out, then some four parts of flour are strewn on it. With lukewarm tap water, the old dough and the fresh flour are mixed right in the bowl for a new supply. At the right temperature (room temperature) the sourdough is ready the next day. Sourdough made of rye flour works best.

TIP!

Put the fresh sourdough in a larger bowl. If it overflows, it is easily cleaned up.

When baking bread, regulating the heat is not so simple, for the bread isolates, because of its loosely constituted dough and the air enclosed in it. The heat penetrates to the center of the loaf with difficulty to bake the dough through from there. It is even worse to heat the Dutch oven from below with too many coals. Even with the 14 size, four to six coals under the pot are quite enough to bake the bread. As many coals as will fit loosely can go on the lid.

1.

2.

Baking with yeast is so simple:

1. Put the rolls in the Dutch oven, which is well dusted with flour, and put it on the fire. The temperature should not exceec 122 degrees Fahrenheit.

2. After rising, the rolls have doubled in volume; then you can bake them.

3. Bake slowly and without too much lower heat, until you can stick a toothpick in and it comes out of the bread clean.

4. The individual rolls can be separated easily.

3.

4.

Cowboy Sourdough Rolls

Rolls made of sourdough—the ideal baked goods for the Dutch oven, rather like a kind of cakes.

½	cup	sourdough starter	½	tsp.	natron
1	cup	milk			barely 1 tsp. salt
1	cup	flour	1	tbsp.	sugar
1	tsp.	baking powder			butter

First start the sourdough with milk and a cup of flour and let it set about eight hours in a warm place. Then add the rest of the flour mixed with the other ingredients and knead into the dough.

Roll the dough out about finger-thick and cut into equal squares. Melt the butter in the lid of the Dutch oven and roll the rolls in the melted butter from both sides.

Then put them into the greased Dutch oven and let them rise half an hour with four to six coals on the lid. Then bake about half an hour over medium heat.

Sourdough Pancakes

Traditionally served with crisp-fried bacon and maple syrup [or sausage!].

2	cups	sourdough starter (fed the previous day, already bubbly, of best rye flour)	1		slightly beaten egg
1	cup	wheat flour	2	tsp.	oil
1	cup	water or milk	2	tsp.	sugar
					oil or plant fat for baking

Mix the ingredients well in a bowl with a fork and put aside in a warm place for an hour, until the dough is good and bubbly. To bake, put spoonfuls of the dough into the hot lid with the butter. Bake briefly from one side, then turn and bake brown from the other side. The pancakes are incomparably light and have a delicate sourdough taste.

The pancakes are really successful when they are as big as a beer coaster and as thick as a little finger. For this, the dough must have the right consistency. If it is too liquid, the pancakes will be too big and flat. If the dough is too tough, the pancakes will be too thick and will not bake through properly. Turn the pancakes when bubbles arise from the middle of the dough and the underside is brown.

This recipe is good for a fairly large number of pancakes, thus you might want to halve the recipe but retain the egg all the same. In no case should you return the dough to the sourdough. It would go bad at once, since the oil and egg are mixed into it. If the taste is too sour for you, the dough can be sweetened with a teaspoon of natron.

Sourdough Rye Rolls

Certainly you can bake real bread in a Dutch oven, but for simplicity and ease it is usually rolls that are made, naturally, of an essentially heartier sourdough.

The sourdough for these rolls is made only of rye flour. When baking, wheat flour is added to enhance the baking process. This recipe was the basic nourishment for trappers in the USA.

2	cups	sourdough
2	cups	rye flour
2	cups	white flour
1	pack	dry yeast
1	tsp.	salt
1	pinch	sugar

lukewarm water

flour for rolling out

alternatively, 1 pack baking powder and 1 tsp. natron instead of the yeast and sugar

Finished sourdough rye rolls, less full-bodied than bread.

First revive the sourdough: Take the sourdough (about two cups) out of the refrigerator, put in a large bowl, and make into a thickly fluid dough along with the two cups of rye flour and the lukewarm water. Cover and let stand overnight in a warm place.

On the next day mix the dry yeast with the wheat flour, salt, and sugar in a bowl, add two cups of sourdough from the previous day, add buttermilk, and knead to a dough that no longer sticks to the bowl or your fingers.

Make a lump of the yeast dough and let it rise in the bowl for an hour, until its volume has doubled. Whoever uses baking powder instead of yeast will skip this step.

Put the dough in the Dutch oven over a campfire and let it rise an hour with a few coals on the lid. When the dough has doubled, knead it into a roll, but not too much, so the air bubbles will not be removed.

Cut the dough with a knife into eight roughly equal big rolls, and put them in the Dutch oven in a ring shape. Do not knead the cut-off pieces of dough, since they will rise badly, being made of rye flour. Put them in the Dutch oven with plenty of flour and warm them with coals on the lid for an hour, so they can rise a second time.

To bake, put 1/4 to 1/3 of the coals under the Dutch oven and the rest on the lid. Check after 20 minutes to see what the rolls are doing.

Yeast Rolls

For a 10 Dutch Oven; ingredients for 10 to 12 rolls

4	cups	flour
1	cube	yeast
1/8	cup	warm water
		some oil
		salt

After the first rising, add:

as you wish, bacon cubes, fried onions, sunflower seeds, herbs (cumin, sesame, dry herbs ...)

Mix well the ingredients for the basic dough and knead it. Then put the dough in a pot, cover with a hand towel, and let rise for half an hour at room-temperature.

Only now should you work the other ingredients (bacon and onions go very well) into the dough. Divide the dough, thus prepared, into twelve equally large balls and dust them individually with some flour so they don't stick together while baking.

Now put the dough balls in the Dutch oven with gaps between them, and then put the oven on the coals. Baking takes 40 to 50 minutes, when the coals are already hot. To reach 350 degrees Fahrenheit you need about seven coals under the pot and 14 on the lid.

A final tip: If you sprinkle some ground cheese on the rolls about ten minutes before they are done, you'll have cheese roles like those from the baker.

Yeast rolls are easy to make.

Olive Bread

For about six people		
1¾	cups	flour (light)
4		eggs
½	cup	olive oil
½	cup	white wine
1	tsp.	salt
1	tsp.	baking powder
		Garlic to taste
¼	lb.	fresh cheese
¼	lb.	cooked ham
20		black olives, pitted
20		green olives, pitted

Mix the flour, eggs, salt, olive oil, white wine, and baking powder, and work into a good dough. Cut the cheese and ham small and mix into the dough. Halve the olives and work them in. Form the dough into one or two flat cakes (to fit the Dutch oven), put into the oven, which is greased with olive oil, and bake some 30 minutes.

Olive bread goes very well with seasoned meat dishes, casseroles, or as small bite-size morsels with a glass of well-chilled Retsina.

Bread with Guaranteed Success

For a 12 Dutch Oven

Choose a bread mixture you want (ciabatta or rye bread with yeast would be very suitable) that is available in 1-pound packages. Prepare by following the directions on the package and let it rise in a bowl for half an hour. Then knead the dough a little with floured hands on a floured surface (so as not to ruin the already developed bubbles in the dough) and form a roll. Cut it with a knife into two equal pieces, cut them in two and again in two, so you have eight nearly equally large pieces of dough. Form them into balls; don't knead them much.

To prepare the Dutch oven for baking, grease the bottom and walls and flour the bottom. Then put the first dough ball in the middle and the other seven around it at equal distances. The balls should not touch.

To let the dough rise again, put on the lid and put four coals on it. The dough usually must rise another 30 to 40 minutes. Turn the lid a little every few minutes so the warmth—not heat—radiates evenly.

To bake the bread, heat the Dutch oven for 15 minutes with nine coals below and 15 on the lid. Then remove four coals from below and put them on the lid for another 15 minutes of baking. By then the bread must be far enough along so you can make the first test. The bread (depending on the kind) should have a golden yellow to dark brown surface. Stick a long fork or needle through the bread from the top to the bottom of the Dutch oven. Feel the thickness of the crust, the consistency of the dough, and the thickness of the bottom, which scorches easily.

The bread is done when you can pull the needle back out and no bits of dough stick to it, or when you knock on the bread and it sounds hollow.

The finished bread can normally be taken out of the Dutch oven easily and put on a rack to cool.

Two ciabatta loaves from a baking mixture, baked in a 14 Dutch oven.

Beer Bread

A very simple kind of bread to bake in camp. It works in an 8, 10 or 12 Dutch oven. With a 12 oven, put 15 charcoal briquettes on the lid and 8 under the pot.

3	cups	flour
1	bottle	beer
1	tsp.	baking powder
1	tsp.	sugar
½	tsp.	salt
1	tsp.	onion salt

If you want:

¼	tsp.	dried chili peppers
¼	tsp.	garlic powder

The preparation is very simple. Mix all the dry ingredients and pour in the beer till a firm dough results. Now stop kneading. The baking powder starts to work when it is wet. The longer one kneads, the more the baking powder evaporates.

Form a ball, grease the Dutch oven with olive oil, and dust with flour. Put the dough ball in the Dutch oven and press it flat. With a very sharp knife, cut into the dough surface crosswise.

After 20 to 25 minutes, the bread should be done. The surface is then brown and the bread sounds hollow when you rap on it.

CAKE

TIP!

Cake pans made of metal fit into the various sizes of Dutch ovens. So they don't touch the bottom, make individual cherry-size balls of aluminum foil. Put three or four of them in the Dutch oven and put the cake pan on them to keep them from touching the hot bottom.

Pineapple Upside-Down Cake

The Dutch oven is also suitable for making desserts. Here is a simple recipe for a pineapple upside-down cake. The trick is to layer the fruit at the bottom of the pot and cover it with the dough. After baking, it is turned over, hence its name.

For a 10 Dutch Oven		
1	can	pineapple
1	tsp.	butter
2	tbsp.	sugar
1	pack	prepared dough

Line the Dutch oven with a double layer of aluminum foil, put the pot on the fire, and melt the butter in the foil. Sprinkle the sugar on it and then distribute the fruit without the liquid. Prepare the dough as directed, but instead of three eggs (usually called for) use only one.

Put the dough over the fruit by the spoonful, so it fills in the pot evenly. Put on the lid and heat the Dutch oven with seven briquettes below and 13 on the lid. After 20 minutes, the cake should be almost done. Open the lid and test the dough with a toothpick.

Bake the cake golden brown and then let it cool a bit in the Dutch oven. Carefully grip the foil with your fingertips and lift the cake out of the pot. The foil should not be damaged in this action.

Now the cake is turned. To do this, cover the bottom (which is now on top!) with a plate, slide a second plate under the cake, and turn both plates 180 degrees so that the lower one is on top. Voila! Remove the foil and enjoy the cake.

Pineapple upside-down cake.

Cinnamon Buns

For ten to twelve pieces in a 14 Dutch oven. To make them in a 16 Dutch oven, double the dough recipe but not the filling. Just make it somewhat more liquidy.

For the dough:

4	cups	flour
1	cube	yeast
1	tsp.	sugar
1	cup	milk
4	tbsp.	sugar
4	tbsp.	butter
1	pinch	salt

For the filling:

8	tbsp.	melted butter
1	tbsp.	cinnamon
1	cup	brown sugar
3	tbsp.	cocoa powder
2	cups	shredded chocolate
1	cup	raisins
		Rum

A Dutch oven full of cinnamon pastries looks not only tasty but spectacular!

Dissolve the yeast and the sugar in a cup of warm milk. Put the flour in a bowl. Make a pit in the middle and add the dissolved yeast there. Work the yeast under from the edges and add the rest of the milk until a pre-dough forms; let it rise ten minutes. Then add the other ingredients and mix well until the dough lets go of the bowl and is firm and supple. Then let the dough rise an hour until it is twice as high.

Roll the dough out flat and coat with the filling. Then roll it up and slice it. Put the slices side by side in the greased Dutch oven.

There the dough must rise again until it doubles again. It is best to put baking paper at the bottom of the Dutch oven, rising up on the sides so one can remove the rolls easily. Before baking, paint the pastries with egg yolk.

Bake the pastries to a golden yellow for 30 to 40 minutes with little heat below and much heat on the lid.

Pear Cake

For about four people

Dough:

8	tbsp.	flour
4	tbsp.	sugar
1	pack	vanilla sugar
1	cup	whipped cream

Filling:

4		large pears
4	tbsp.	butter
3	tbsp.	sugar
		juice of a lemon
½	cup	fresh cream

Line the Dutch oven with aluminum foil with the shining side showing. Make a dough with flour, sugar, vanilla sugar, and cream, and put aside to settle. Meanwhile peel the pears, remove the seeds, and cut into thick slices.

Put butter on the foil, add sugar and lemon juice, and steam the pear halves in them. Arrange the pear slices in a star and spread the raised dough over them. Put on the lid and back approx. 15 minutes. Then lift out with aluminum foil.

Mix the fresh cream with some vanilla sugar and put a blob on each portion of the tart.

QUICHE

For two pieces, for a 14 Dutch Oven

For the dough:

2	cups	flour
1	pack	dry yeast
2	tsp.	sugar
1	cup	buttermilk
1	tsp.	salt
3½	tbsp.	melted butter

For the filling:

1	lb.	onions
1	lb.	leek
1	lb.	cooked ham
7	tbsp.	butter
4	cups	cream-thick milk, each ¾ cup
5		eggs
¼	cup	flour

Put the flour in a bowl, mix with dry yeast and sugar, add the lukewarm buttermilk, and mix. Cover the bowl with a cloth and let rise for 20 minutes.

Since two quiches are to be made from the dough, divide it and put one half in the refrigerator for half an hour. Thus the second dough is ready when the first is baking.

Knead the first dough portion again and let it rise half an hour.
Meanwhile prepare the filling: Cut the onions and leeks into fine rings and the ham into fine strips. Heat the butter in the Dutch oven and brown the leeks with the onions and ham strips. Take out of the Dutch oven and season in a bowl.

Beat the cream-thick milk with the eggs and flour and season with pepper and salt.

Roll the dough out thin and lay it out in the buttered Dutch oven so that it is at least a fingerbreadth high at the edge. Spread half the vegetable mixture evenly on the dough and pour half the milk mixture on it. Be sure that the fluid does not run under the dough.

Bake it in the Dutch oven about 20 minutes, 10 minutes with 10 coals under the pot and 18 on the lid, then another 10 minutes with only 5 coals below and the rest on the lid.

When the first quiche is baked, take the second dough portion out of the refrigerator and let it rise.

Waffle Mix

6		eggs
~2	cups	milk
1	cup	cream
		sugar
		flour

Stir the eggs, milk, cream, and sugar together briefly. Then gradually add flour until the dough it thick but fluid. Bake on both sides in the lid of the Dutch oven.

VARIOUS

Brown Cabbage Hike

The right recipe for a brown cabbage hike, that your guests will long remember. Make a fire at the meeting point and meet your happy wanderers there. When the fire has died down, put the Dutch oven in the fire and go on your hike. When you come back two hours later, the brown cabbage will be ready, and you need only brown the prepared fried potatoes. After 15 minutes every hungry hiker has his food hot on the plate.

For the Dutch Oven
fat
onion cubes
brown cabbage (green cabbage) from a can or freshly cooked in advance
broth
loose, spicy sausages (Bregenwurst) from a can

Per Person		
1		smoked pork sausages or spicy sausages (Bregenwurst) (if you can get it)
1	slice	bacon
1	slice	smoked pork chops
1	slice	smoked bacon

Put a good blob of fat in the Dutch oven, steam the onions in it, add the brown cabbage, and pour the broth over it. If it is not yet seasoned, salt and pepper it now and flavor with some clove powder. Take the spicy sausages (Bregenwurst) out of the can and mix it into the brown cabbage. Put the smoked pork sausages, spicy sausages (Bregenwurst), and meat slices under the brown cabbage. Put the pot in the hot coals with little upper heat. Remember, "Brown cabbage must gleam like a freshly plowed field!"

Bacon and spicy sausages (Bregenwurst) are suitable additions, and if space is short, they can be cooked in a pot. They do not taste so good warmed up. So if you have a tripod with a kettle, you can also prepare cooked frankfurters and bacon. Flavor them with pepper, salt, ketchup, and mustard.

For fried potatoes out of the pan, per person		
½	cup	bacon cubes
½	cup	onion cubes
2	cups	cooked potatoes
		dried marjoram, cumin powder
		pepper and salt

Making tasty fried potatoes is an art that is easy to learn. It is important that good frying potatoes be fatty. Take as big a pan as you can or a big Dutch oven (not the lid–that has no rim).

Heat a lot of fat in the pan and add the bacon cubes. Brown them glassy.

Now come the sliced potatoes. To make them good and brown, the pan must be big enough so each piece has enough contact with the hot bottom. Now it is important to swing the pan well or stir the potatoes sufficiently if the pan is too heavy. When the potatoes are brown, add the onions–not sooner, or they'll burn!

As soon as the onions turn glassy, season with pepper and salt, a little cumin powder, and a lot of marjoram–more than you think. This spice goes very well with fried potatoes.

Everybody comes with his plate and receives a blob of brown cabbage, a smoked pork sausages, a spicy sausage (Bregenwurst), a slice of bacon, and smoked pork. If there is still room on the plate, it can be carefully filled with fried potatoes.

Dutch Oven Pizza

For the dough:

1	lb.	all-purpose flour, baking-strong
3	tbsp.	fresh yeast (= one cube) or a pack of dry yeast
1½	tbsp.	sugar
1	cup	lukewarm water
3	tbsp.	olive oil
2	tsp.	salt

For the sauce:

1	can	pizza tomatoes
		pepper and oregano

For the topping:

ground cheese

ingredients to taste: onions, pepperoni, mushrooms, olives, etc.

Sieve the flour into a bowl, make a pit in the middle and add the crumbled yeast, sugar, and water. Knead and set aside in a warm place to rise for half an hour. Then add salt and olive oil and knead strongly. Make apple-size balls of the dough and roll them out, bend the edge up slightly so the topping doesn't flow under the dough. Then top to taste.

First spread the tomato sauce of pureed tomatoes from a can (pizza tomatoes), season with oregano and pepper, and spread (thinly) on the dough. Then add all the toppings except fresh mushrooms or salami and sprinkle oregano liberally over them. Finally put the mushrooms and salami on the cheese.

The pizza is done when the dough rim is light brown and no longer bends through. Bake it with a lot of upper heat.

TIPS!

Put the lid of the Dutch oven on the lid rack and put the pot on the lid with its legs up. Thus you can take the pizza out more easily than by having to lift it out of the deep Dutch oven.

Cut two strips approx. 2" wide out of parchment paper. Put them crosswise under the pizza, reaching up to just under the lid. To remove the pizza, just lift it by the paper strips.

Salt and yeast must never come together in the bowl, since the salt kills the yeast!

ALSATIAN FLAME CAKE

Flame cakes are very thin flat cakes topped with bacon and onions. The quantities vary depending on how thin the dough is rolled and how many flame cakes are to be made. It is important that the flame cake have a very thin base and not much topping.

For baking, the flame cake is put into an extremely hot Dutch oven—put as many coals on the lid as will fit. It is also quite possible to put the lid on its rack and the pot upside down on the lid, but this is unhandy.

For the dough:

2	cups	flour
3	tbsp.	fresh yeast
1	tsp.	sugar
1¼	cups	lukewarm water
3	tbsp.	olive oil
2	tsp.	salt

For the topping:

2	cups	fresh cream
1	cup	curds
		pepper and salt
½	lb.	finely cubed smoked bacon
3		onions, cut into very fine rings

Alsatian Flame Cake

Mix a thin, fluid dough of yeast, lukewarm milk, and sugar, with all other ingredients except the water kneaded with the kneading hook. Add water until the dough loosens from the bowl. Make the dough into a ball, dust with flour and leave in the bowl, covered with a hand towel, to rise for an hour, until the dough has doubled.

Depending on the size of the Dutch oven, take out balls of dough and roll them out as thin as the back of a knife, dust with plenty of flour and put on the topping.

For the topping, beat the fresh cream and the curds in a bowl and season with salt and pepper. Spread several spoons of this mixture on the flame cake and scatter the small rings of onion and the bacon cubes over it. Bake over high heat in a few minutes.

Popcorn

fat for the pot
popcorn kernels
salt or sugar to taste

Cover the bottom of the Dutch oven with oil and heat with plenty of lower heat. Scatter the popcorn in it, so that there is only one layer in the pot and every kernel contacts the bottom. Put on the lid and wait until the popping stops. You may want to stir occasionally with a wooden spoon. Take the popcorn out of the pot and sprinkle with salt or sugar in a pot.

1. You must not put more popcorn in the pot; otherwise it will scorch.

2. After a short time the chowhounds can dig in.

Dutch Oven Fondue

The manifold preparation possibilities are what make the Dutch oven so attractive. The black pot is also a fondue pot that can be filled with fat or broth. Instead of using the tiny fondue forks, with which one risks starving to death, it is recommended that several shashlik skewers are prepared for each person, as several pieces of meat at a time can be fried on them. The fondue with broth does not spatter as much as that with fat, and the broth can also be used in other ways.

One reckons on some half pound of meat per person (fillet of lamb, pork, beef or turkey), with four people fitting around a pot; otherwise the arrangement of the skewers will be difficult.

Sides: baked potatoes in foil, olive bread or flatbread go with both variants.

Dutch Oven Paella

For a 12 Dutch Oven					
8		Venus mussels or 2lbs. mussels	3	cups	chicken broth
12		shrimps	2	cups	rice
5		chicken thighs	1		small can artichoke hearts
1		onion	1	cup	peas
1		red chili pepper	½	cup	cubed olives
1		large garlic clove			saffron, paprika, oregano
½	cup	olive oil			pepper and salt
2		tomatoes			

Heat the olive oil in the Dutch oven. Brown the skinned chicken thighs about 15 minutes and then take them out of the oven. Sautee the pressed garlic, cubed onion, washed and cut chili pepper, and tomatoes in the Dutch oven for several minutes. Add the chicken, water, broth, and other spices, and cook for ten minutes.

Add the rice and boil it briefly. Add the washed and shelled shrimp, mussels, artichoke hearts, and peas, and cook with the lid on until the mussels open.

Uncover the paella and stir thoroughly so excess fluid evaporates.

Whoever doesn't want the mussel shells in the paella can cook the mussels separately, remove the shells and just add the mussel meat shortly before serving.

Side: White bread.

Dutch Oven Carbonara

A simple pasta dish that can fill four hungry people.

1	lb.	noodles (better Macaroni than spaghetti)	½	lb.	rib bacon
¼	lb.	parmesan	1	cup	cream
¼	lb.	shredded cheese for baking	4		eggs
					olive oil
					pepper and salt

Cook the noodles in the Dutch oven with plenty of salt water until done, drain, and put aside. Brown the bacon cubes in olive oil in the Dutch oven. Put the noodles back in and mix well. Mix the cream with the four eggs, ground parmesan, plenty of pepper and salt, and pour it over the noodles. Mix briefly, sprinkle with the shredded cheese, and bake with only upper heat until the cheese has turned brown in some places and the egg material has solidified.

Chestnuts

A simple but tasty snack for outdoors.

Chestnuts (about 1 pound in a 10 Dutch oven)
Fat for the pot

Cut the chestnuts with a carpet knife and a lot of caution to cut through ¾ inches of the brown shell at the fuzzy end. Heat the fat in the Dutch oven with as many coals as will fit under it and roast the unshelled chestnuts until the cut opens and they are soft inside. That takes at least 20 minutes. Then "pull your chestnuts out of the fire," wipe off the fat with a cloth, shell them by hand, and eat them while warm.

The chestnuts can also be roasted without fat, but with little lower heat and the lid on, with plenty of coals on it.

Chestnuts not only warm the stomach, but also the fingers in autumn and winter!

Armadillo Eggs

This hearty dish is a little snack or appetizer. Armadillos are the armored animals that live in Texas and New Mexico. They look as if they came from another world.

2		large jars of hot jalapeno peppers; it is important that they are the short, thick ones, not the very long peppers. They should be very spicy!
2	cups	flour
1	tsp.	baking powder
½	lb.	ground mozzarella
2	lbs.	bratwurst fat
2	cups	breadcrumbs mixed with two teaspoons of the Cajun spice mixture noted elsewhere (see p. 166)
1		egg

Cut off the stem ends of the dried peppers and remove the seeds. Fill the hulls with a little cheese. Mix the bratwurst fat, flour, baking powder, and the other half of the cheese to a firm dough. Make small dough plates as big as a beer coaster of this dough.

In the middle of each piece of dough put a pepper. Then wrap the dough completely around the pepper. Dip the individual dough forms first into an egg and then in spiced breadcrumbs. Bake the armadillo eggs with a lot of fat. Heat a lot of fat for this in the Dutch oven.

With them, it is best to serve many cold drinks.

Mexican Dutch Oven Dip

2	cans	kidney beans
4	cups	cheese (cheddar goes very well)
1	cup	mayonnaise
1	cup	sour cream
1	cup	chili sauce
1	cup	pitted olives
		tortilla chips

Sieve the two cans of kidney beans and reduce them to a fine mass in the blender. In the Dutch oven—perhaps lined with thick aluminum foil—first spread the beans on the bottom. Mix the mayonnaise and sour cream and pour over the beans. Add chili sauce, cut the black or green olives into slices, and layer over the sauce. Scatter sharp shredded cheese over it all.

Bake the dish with plenty of heat on the lid for 30 minutes.

To serve, simply put the Dutch oven on the table and let everyone serve himself tortilla chips for dipping.

Honey Mustard Dip

2	cups	mayonnaise
½	cup	mustard
¼	cup	honey
2	squirts	Tabasco

Mix all ingredients well and put in the refrigerator for several hours to blend.

Cajun Spices

The following seasoning is very simple to make and very well suited to giving grilled meat or chicken the right zing.

3	tsp.	salt
2	tsp.	paprika powder
1	tsp.	Cayenne pepper
1	tsp.	black pepper
1	tsp.	onion powder
1	tsp.	garlic powder

Mix the spices and salt and put in a tightly sealing can.

For example, to season chicken with it, mix two teaspoons of this mixture with two cups of breadcrumbs. The chicken pieces are breaded as usual and take on a nice red-brown color and the typical Cajun flavor.

Barbeque Sauce

1	cup	cold coffee
1	cup	Worcestershire sauce
1	cup	ketchup
1	cup	vinegar
2	tsp.	chili powder
2	tsp.	salt
2	cups	onions, chopped fine
½	cup	chili peppers, freshly pureed
6		garlic cloves, pressed
		Tabasco to taste

Simmer all the ingredients in a small Dutch oven at least 20 minutes. It is best to puree the mixture in a blender afterward. It lasts several weeks in the refrigerator.

Baked Camembert

A nice appetizer that one might never expect from a Dutch oven.

1	Camembert
	leaf dough
	cranberries from a jar

Spread out to dough so that it covers the Camembert well. Line the Dutch oven with several layers of aluminum foil.

Put the Camembert in the middle of the dough, scatter cranberries over it, and fold the dough together over the Camembert. A hole should remain on top so the moisture can leave and the dough will become crispy.

Brush the dough with egg yolk and bake in the Dutch oven a quarter hour, until the dough is a golden yellow and the cheese has run.

The cheese is packed in the dough.

After a few minutes the dough is baked and the cheese is liquid.

Baked Feta

An appetizer for four people		
1	pack	feta cheese
2	tbsp.	olive oil
1		garlic clove
1		hot pepper
1		onion
		black olives
		oregano
		pepper and salt
		thyme
		aluminum foil

Chop the garlic clove roughly and rub some salt on it with the knife, put in a cup, and mix with the olive oil.

The cheese can be baked in a single pan or by portions. For small portion pans, simply put several layers of foil over a bowl of the right size, and use this for shaping.

Pack the cheese into the foil in two pieces. These pieces should be cut lengthwise again, so they are only half as thick. That makes one portion. Brush the cheeses with the garlic-oil mixture from both sides and put them in the pans. Put the rings of pepper and onion, the olives, and spices over them. Bake the portions 10 to 15 minutes with little lower and almost exclusively upper heat.

You can also put this cheese on larger foil pieces and then fold the foil to bake it in the heat. Then, of course, they must be turned.

DESSERT

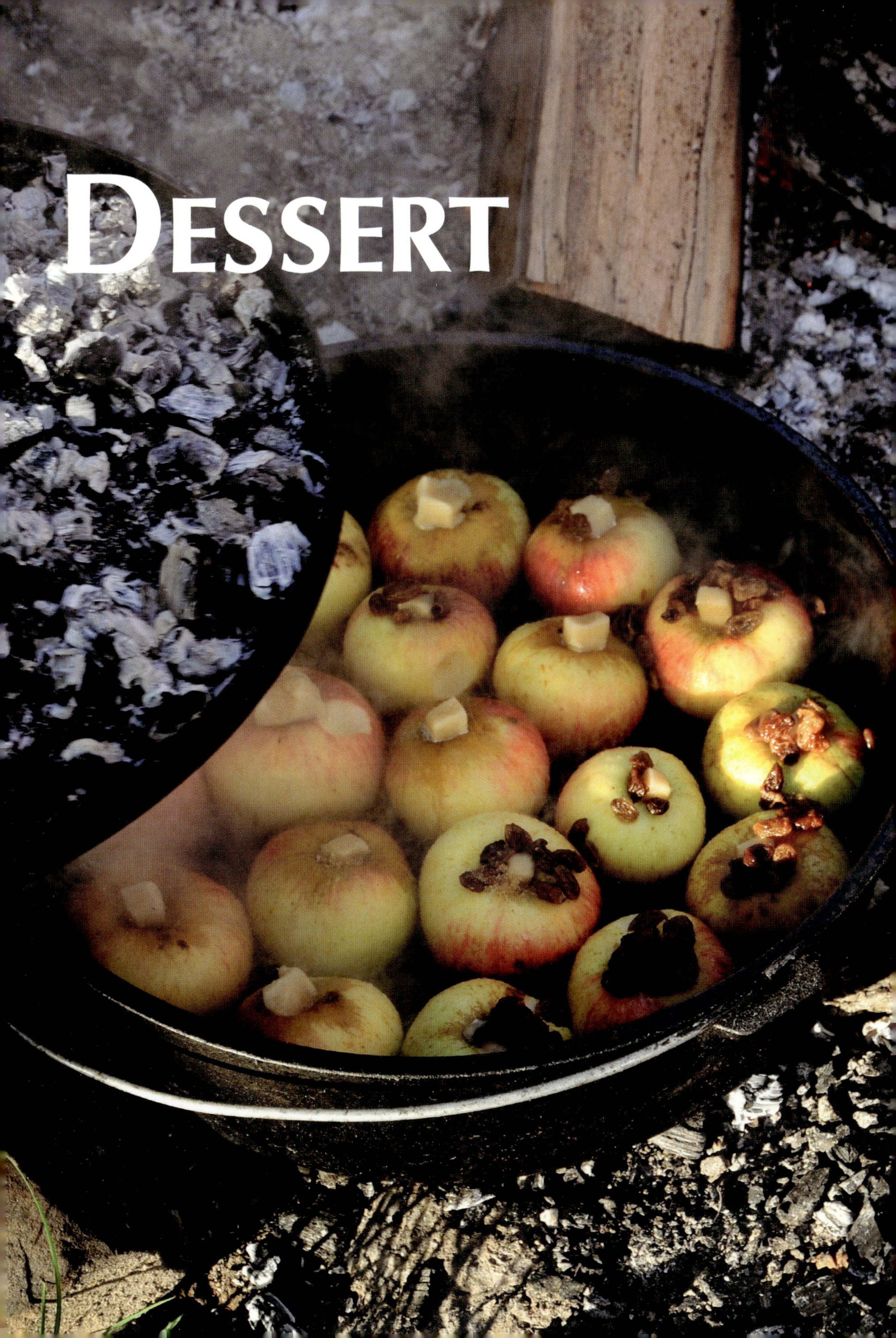

Baked Apples

1		apple per person
1	tbsp.	raisins, chopped almonds, brown sugar (or honey) per apple
		rum
		butter
alternative filling:		
2		marzipan potatoes or raw marzipan

Core the apples with a corer and fill them with the marzipan mixture rolled into a "sausage." Put several soaked raisins on the apples and sprinkle with sugar. Bake in the Dutch oven with some water–so nothing scorches–using upper and lower heat, until the skin splits and the apples are soft.

Since the apples vary in size and structure, one cannot give an exact time. Experience says this is between 10 and 30 minutes. It is advantageous to line the Dutch oven with aluminum foil. Vanilla sauce or vanilla ice cream can go on top of the apples.

TIP!

You can also bake the apples on a grill right next to the goose or duck, but put them on only at the end, as they will be ready too soon otherwise.

COBBLER

This is *the* Dutch-oven dessert! Unbelievably easy to prepare and a hit with children and adults who like to snack.

For an 8 or 10 Dutch Oven		
1	mix	fruitcake or pastry
1	big can	tart peaches (also tastes good with peaches, pears, mixed fruit, etc.)
		brown sugar for sprinkling
		butter
		peach liqueur

Open the peach can and pour all contents into the Dutch oven. Open the baking mixture and scatter the dry mixture—right out of the package—over the peaches. Do not stir at all! That is done later during the "bubbling" while cooking.

Put chips of butter on the bake mixture and sprinkle the brown sugar over it. Bake 15-20 minutes with little lower and much upper heat, until the surface turns brown.

Cobbler from a baking mix.

If you don't want to use baking mix, mix the dough yourself:

For two to three people and one 8 Dutch Oven					
10	tbsp.	flour	½	cup	milk or buttermilk
4	tbsp.	sugar	4	tbsp.	melted butter
½	tsp.	salt	1	can	peaches
1	tsp.	baking powder			

For four to six people and a 12 Dutch Oven

2		large cans peaches, but only the fruit, not the juice from the can, otherwise it will be too liquidy
1¼	cups	flour
11	tbsp.	sugar
½	tsp.	salt
2–3	tsp.	baking powder
1	cup	milk or buttermilk
10	tbsp.	melted butter

Mix the dry ingredients, add the milk and melted butter, and stir smooth with a brush. Put the fruits in the Dutch oven, the dough over the fruit in an even layer, and sprinkle with bits of butter and brown sugar. Bake with little lower heat until the fruit boils and then bake more with upper heat until the surface develops a brown crust.

The warm cobbler is very pleasant with peach liqueur and ice.

1. Put the fruit in the Dutch oven and carefully lay the dough over it, so it is evenly thick.

2. Sprinkle well with butter and brown sugar.

3. When the filling has boiled, take the Dutch oven off the fire and bake with only upper heat.

4. The cobbler develops a nice crust and is spooned out of the oven warm and eaten with peach liqueur and vanilla ice cream

Apple Rings

A small 8 Dutch Oven suffices to fry it.		
1½	lbs.	plant fat for frying
4		large apples
4	tbsp.	sugar
¼	cup	rum
1	cup	flour
3		eggs
1	cup	milk
		salt
1	tsp.	cinnamon

Peel the apples, remove the cores, and cut into slices about 1/4″ thick. Drip with sugar, some cinnamon and rum, and let them set–the longer, the better.

Prepare a dough of flour, eggs, milk, and a pinch of salt. Heat the plant fat in the Dutch oven until it forms small pearls. Dip the individual apple rings in the dough with two forks and let them slide into the fat.

When the underside is golden brown, turn them. Take them out and let them dry on a kitchen towel. Sprinkle with sugar and cinnamon again shortly before serving.

This dessert is well suited for an outdoor day, especially when you pick the apples yourself on a hike.

Elderberry Blossoms in Wine Dough

When the elderberries bloom in the spring and give out their wonderful aroma, one should pick some of the blossoms—naturally in full bloom—around noon on a hot day. Transport them carefully, so that as little pollen as possible is lost.

1	cup	flour
1	tbsp.	sugar
		white wine
		freshly bloomed unwashed elderberry blossoms
		coconut oil
		powdered sugar

Prepare a thin fluid dough or flour, sugar, and white wine, and dip the unwashed (important!) blossoms into it, take out by the stems, and fry them in coconut oil in the Dutch oven. Sprinkle with powdered sugar and serve warm.

Red Wine Pears

Red-wine pears are a wonderful side for wild meat dishes or taste great with vanilla ice cream as a dessert.

For four people and a 10 Dutch Oven					
1		sliced orange	1	bottle	red wine
4		pears	1		cinnamon sprig
1	cup	sugar			

Lay out the Dutch oven with orange slices, peel four pears or apples, and put them on the orange slices. Then pour in a bottle of fruity red wine, put the cinnamon sprig in the red wine, and add plenty of sugar. After 20 minutes of little upper and lower heat, check to see if the pears are soft.

My Open Fire Favorites

a personal Dutch Oven recipe log